THE PANDEMICS WORLD

EPIDEMIC AND SOCIETY, PREPPING FOR OUTBREAK, QUARANTINE AND CLIMATE CHANGE. SIMPLE MANUAL TO PREVENT INFECTION AND PROTECT YOURSELF. PLANNING FOR A 'STATE OF EMERGENCY' WITH A *SMILE*

by Damian P. Brook

professional before attempting any techniques outlined in this book.

By reading this document, the reader agrees that under no circumstances is the author responsible for any losses, direct or indirect, which are incurred as a result of the use of information contained within this document, including, but not limited to, — errors, omissions, or inaccuracies.

This book is dedicated to my future wife... even in serious things
 one must always smile...

"Serious natural disasters call for a change of mindset that
forces to abandon the logic of pure consumerism and promote
respect for creation."
   (Albert Einstein)

"Life is short. Break the rules, forgive quickly, kiss slowly, love
deeply, laugh uncontrollably and never regret what made
you smile."
   (Mark Twain)

Table of Contents

"The crisis is the greatest blessing for people and nations, because the crisis brings progress."

(Albert Einstein)

"A day without a smile is a lost day."

(Charlie Chaplin)

Introduction

As you already know, the strains of viruses that are so named get their names from the nature of their structures and the way they have a crown on their surfaces. The way these viruses behave, the crown spikes are their main means for fusing with the cell of the host (i.e. an animal or human body).

Every coronavirus that has ever infected the human body have structures similar to the other viruses within the family of coronaviruses. In a way, this is both a blessing and a curse for any newly reported cases of this new virus. It is a blessing because, following the earliest mapping of the structure of the first SARS coronavirus in China, subsequent mapping of the new coronaviruses have been much easier because of the similar atomic structures that these new ones have to the first ever recorded coronavirus.

Common cold is caused by a coronavirus and since the structures of these coronaviruses are similar to each other, it also follows that they present the same symptoms in humans and therein lies the curse in the similarity of their structures; you cannot know for sure if you simply have a cold or if you've become infected by the new 2019-nCoV.

So far, known strains of coronaviruses that have attacked humans over time have been grouped into alpha- and beta- coronaviruses for the ones that cause common colds in various regions of the world. An example of the alpha- coronavirus is called 229E and is the most common type of coronavirus that causes the common cold.

The SARS and MERS coronaviruses, however, are described as beta-coronaviruses. These are the second genus level of coronaviruses as far as the group classifications of this family of viruses go. In moving up from alpha-coronavirus to the beta structure, a mutation occurs in the protein structure of these coronaviruses to yield a whole new virus strain.

Where do these coronaviruses come from?

In studies that have been conducted into the origins of these coronaviruses, they seem to have originated from wildlife surrounding the region where these outbreaks are first recorded.

In 2003, the outbreak of the first SARS-CoV was traced back to bats and civets that were present in tropical Asia and sub- Saharan Africa and since then, the coronavirus strains found in all forms of wildlife around the world have been monitored closely for the emergence of new viruses following evolutions or mutations.

The family of CoVs infects a wide variety of animals around the world, causing respiratory infections in these animals as well as enteric and even neurological diseases that can be mild or severe depending on the level of expression of these viruses in the body of the animal host.

In animals, there have been cases of both alpha- and beta-coronaviruses and in most of these animals, the expression of these viruses can be asymptomatic and they can go on carrying these viruses for years without dying of any real illnesses. This ability has been said to make these animals excellent carriers of viruses as well as other lethal disease- causing microorganisms known to man.

Sometimes, the viruses present in these animals become transmissible to humans directly in ways that cause lethal symptoms in human beings that come in contact with the viruses. In such cases, it is believed that the coronaviruses that are already present in these animals mutate (i.e. undergo a change in structure) in a way that allows them to become easily expressed in the bodies of human hosts.

In the studies of the coronavirus cases that have been identified in human beings over time, the virus typically has an incubation period of about 2 to 7 days. Each new coronavirus, however, comes along with its own unique incubation period based on its virulence and so, it has been the case that the more lethal strains of the coronavirus have longer incubation periods as was noticed in the outbreak of MERS in 2012 where some individuals did not have symptoms until about 10 days after their first exposure to the virus.

Some strains of coronaviruses have the ability to be transmitted from one human being to another even when symptoms have not begun to show and this unique characteristic was first noted during the SARS and MERS outbreaks of 2002 and 2012 respectively.

The atomic structure of coronaviruses is described as spherical in nature and contains single-stranded RNA that is positive-sense. This unique nature of the protein structure of the coronavirus is the reason it's so efficient at causing symptoms in many human beings, even if they eventually turn out to be mild symptoms.

As an RNA that is single-stranded and positive-sensed, it means that it can easily merge with the DNA of every host animal and rapidly alter the structure of that DNA as it expresses itself in its own DNA, thus changing the DNA structure of the host animal or human being leading to the expression of physical symptoms.

Another unique feature of the family of coronaviruses is that immunity against these viruses disappears within a year of having suffered and recovered from them, thus leaving you susceptible to a fresh round of attacks if the virus comes around again within your locality. This makes the coronaviruses unique from other virus families such as the ones that cause measles or chickenpox where they leave you immune for as long as a lifetime after you have suffered it once.

The fact that these coronaviruses leave you with little immunity against them after about a year is the reason there won't ever be a shortage of cases of common colds around the world that usually peak during winter and fall months because it is the best time for these coronaviruses to survive and replicate fast.

Through the course of outbreaks of the illnesses caused by the coronavirus, the case has always been that there are no known cures or vaccines that can effectively eliminate the virus forever. For these viruses, they usually resolve on their own after they have been expressed within the body of the host and if you have ever suffered a common cold, you'd know that this was also the case in dealing with the infection; they just go away after some time.

The difference between the common cold and outbreaks of SARS and MERS, however, lies in the fact that the latter two illnesses can lead to death in some of the people that have been diagnosed with those specific strains of coronavirus. The increase in the lethal nature of the mutated viruses has led to the devotion of more resources in the development of vaccines and drugs that can help lower the mortality associated with being diagnosed with the illnesses.

With each new outbreak of a novel strain within the family of coronaviruses, more information is uncovered about the true nature of this family of viruses and the way it affects the human body.

"The virus has taught us one thing: in a world that wants to raise walls, nature has shown us that borders do not exist."

(Maria Rita Gismondo)

"Laugh whenever you can: it's cheap medicine."
(George Gordon Byron)

Chapter : 1
A Brief History

On December 8th 2019, the first patient to be diagnosed with COVID-19 presented symptoms. During the next ten days, doctors identified seven further cases. Only two of those new cases could be directly linked with the outbreak's supposed ground zero, the Huanan Seafood Wholesale Market in Wuhan City. That a new virus had originated from the live animal markets in China, which still provide a perfect breeding ground for new diseases due to their poor hygiene and overcrowded conditions, surprised nobody.

When the Chinese CDC sent a consortium of medical experts to investigate on December 31st, they pinpointed an earlier case, involving a man treated for a similar disease thirty days earlier. In spite of extensive inquiries, no connection between this man and the Huanan Seafood Wholesale Market could be found. As a result, medical experts concluded the outbreak was already extending beyond those initially exposed.

On the same day as the December 31st investigation began, the Chinese CDC notified the World Health Organization of twenty-seven pneumonia cases of unknown cause in Wuhan City, Hubei Province, China. An entire month after the first suspected COVID-19 infection, there were less than thirty cases. Coronaviruses, of which seven exist with potential for transmission between humans, vary greatly in their ability to spread. Given the low number of infections, a consensus within the W.H.O. obviously concluded COVID-19 was not particularly contagious. Subsequently, the W.H.O. responded by specifically not recommending any restrictions on travel or trade. On January 1st 2020, Chinese authorities closed the Huanan Seafood Wholesale Market.

At this point, Western virologists were receiving limited information on what appeared to be a minor outbreak of a new disease. Wuhan City is a huge, congested metropolis with over 11 million residents, so the low number of infections after thirty-one days superficially implied there was no real danger of an epidemic. Although professional experts from around the globe generally concurred with this opinion, offering re-assuring words in public to anyone who would pay, the next thirty days proved them wrong.

Most news coverage on December 31st, sparked by the World Health Organization's involvement, included references to the 2002/3 SARS outbreak. SARS (severe acute respiratory syndrome) is also a coronavirus, and was responsible for the deaths of 774 people. Generally, reporters presented a distant problem in a distant land while emphasizing the comparative weakness of the new virus compared to its more petrifying cousin.

January 9th 2020 saw the first death of an infected patient. The second fatality occurred six days later. By January 19th, 204 confirmed cases existed, and COVID-19 had claimed a third victim. Of those 204 cases, one in Shenzhen along with two more in Beijing proved the virus was spreading throughout China. Medical staff in both Japan and Thailand had, by this time, also identified one infected person each. Neither of those two cases could be connected in any way with the Huanan Seafood Wholesale Market.

No clear pattern for COVID-19 infections was emerging. A neat yet obscure solution, such as eating at the same restaurant or an ambiguous social connection, simply did not exist. Many of those presenting symptoms could not be linked with known carriers in any way. Although cases seemed to appear as if caused by some dark magic, a far more sinister explanation would be found.

Between January 20th and January 30th, the day on which the W.H.O. declared a Public Health Emergency of International Concern, the situation worsened. Detected infections grew slowly yet steadily, rising from 278 to 916 by January 24th. On January 25th, the total cases in mainland China doubled to more than 2,000. The figure then rose daily from 2,700 to 4,400 to 6,000 to 7,700 to 9,700. On January 30th alone, 2,000 new infections were identified, more than had been uncovered during the virus's first 56 days.

As bad as the escalation seemed during this period, the actions of the Chinese government implied the situation would become much worse. On January 23rd, the Hubei lockdowns, a unique event in modern history, began. At two am, an official notice informed residents about the suspension of all public transport services from ten am. The Wuhan airport, metro stations, and trains stations were subsequently closed. Without specific permission from the authorities, any form of travel beyond the city's borders was forbidden. Widespread public panic ensued as eleven million people found themselves trapped with a killer virus.

At a press conference held by the Chinese government on January 26th, the head of China's National Health Commission, Ma Xiaowei, offered a belated justification for the Hubei lockdowns. He unequivocally stated COVID-19 was infectious during its incubation period, which could last between ten and fourteen days.

His disclosure almost certainly caused numerous sharp intakes of breath from experts around the globe. SARS had been contained with relative ease because the disease could not be passed on until symptoms were present. COVID-19, like the common cold, was being spread by those who did not even know they were infected. If carriers could not be quarantined, an epidemic would inevitably follow. To the Chinese government, a lockdown of almost everyone who could have been exposed to the virus offered the only plausible solution.

On January 31st, China's officials reported the existence of 1,500 new confirmed cases on the mainland, bringing the total to 11,200. Researchers from Hong Kong responded by estimating the figure for Wuhan alone was actually 75,815.

Exactly one month after the W.H.O. notification, COVID-19 had claimed over 200 lives. Infection numbers were still growing, but unofficial sources claimed the daily increases were being artificially limited by the testing capacity of the medical services. More than sixty Million people had been in lockdown for as long as eight days, trapped at home with nothing to do but fearfully wait. Videos of packed hospitals abounded on social media.

On that same day, the US Department of Health and Human Services declared a Public Health Emergency. The CDC also issued its first quarantine order for more than 50 years, responding to six out of 241 potentially infected people testing positive for COVID-19 on returning from China. In England, the first two confirmed virus patients were transferred to a specialist infection unit in Newcastle. Sixty-two countries were now enforcing special immigration controls on Chinese citizens.

Western governments, feeling mislead and ill-used, are already accusing the Chinese authorities of lying, massaging the figures to prevent panic. Thirty-one days after the first fatality, more than 1,000 people have died.

In Wenzhou, a city of 9 million residents, the lockdown should have ended yesterday but still remains in force. Only one person per household is allowed to go outside just once every two days. The areas in lockdown are dark zones, shrouded in secrecy. Social media is heavily censored or even completely blocked. Journalists have gone missing, fuelling rumors of death pits and food shortages. For those confined to their homes, the truth, like the virus, is somewhere out there yet just as ominous, just as insubstantial, just as terrifying.

China's economy is suffering as a direct result of COVID-19. With the world's factory closed for business, companies such as Apple and Tesla are becoming concerned over future product supply. In spite of business pressure from both without and within, workers from Wuhan did not return to their jobs today as expected. The SSE Composite Index, which includes all stocks traded on the Shanghai Stock Exchange, has fallen 7% in less than a month.

For the Chinese government, the first priority is stopping the virus at any cost. If COVID-19 is not contained, they know their country could spiral into chaos. As outside observers, we can only wonder just how far they will go to reach their goal. Personally, I fear for those in the lockdown zones, and desperately hope the most cost-efficient cure for the Wuhan Coronavirus does not become a bullet to the head.

Yet we still have much to learn from China. The infection figures in particular can teach us how COVID-19 spreads. From one case to twenty-seven in the first month. From twenty-seven to 11,200 in the second month. From 11,200 to 42,000+ in the first ten days of the third month. If we accept these numbers are genuine, rather than gross understatements, the trend is still clear.

On January 21st 2020, the first case of COVID-19 on American soil was diagnosed in Washington. Subsequently, thirteen infections have been identified in Illinois, California, Arizona, Massachusetts, and Wisconsin. Although the UK's first confirmed case did not occur until January 31st, there are now eight.

Thirteen people from 327 million together with eight people from 68 million. The figures seem ridiculously low, and certainly no cause for concern. China thought the same thing as they went from one to twenty-seven confirmed cases out of

> billion people in the first month. Less than forty days later, entire cities are quarantined, but the virus keeps spreading.

To make an informed decision, you will need to understand just how the virus works. To quote Sun Tzu, you must know your enemy.

"The real crisis is the crisis of incompetence. 'Inconvenience of people and nations is the laziness in seeking solutions and ways out."

(Albert Einstein)

"The art of life is learning to suffer and learning to smile."
(Hermann Hesse)

Chapter : 2
Business Risk and Continuity Planning

During the peak of an infectious disease outbreak, business should expect a disruption in their production and supply of goods, services and sales. A well-considered Continuity Plan might strive to adopt an "All Hazards Approach". This approach focuses on how to continue operations, if possible, and to recover services following the novel coronavirus outbreak in the USA if and when it occurs. The more preparation you complete in advance of such a disruption, the more smoothly your business operations will be, and the less risk of business continuity (and cash flow!) disruption.

Develop a pandemic preparedness plan

Developing a generic pandemic business plan in advance will help your company continue operations, communicate effectively, predetermine what programs the company will keep in place during a crisis, set out the budgeting guidelines and decision-making process, and assign responsibility for implementing the pandemic programs that you have developed. It should also include a communication plan, a safety plan, security measures for your physical location(s), supply-chain issues, as well as investor and stakeholder relations. Remember that leaders in your organization may become compromised, and so clarifying chain of command and transfer of power and responsibility processes should be included.

Communications Plan:

Using existing platforms such a cloud services (such as Google drive), internet conferencing, group messaging services such as "What's App", and of course cell phones and email or call lists can help your business to continue almost seamlessly during an outbreak. The key is having a plan and implementing it prior to the event. As an example, trying to set-up a video conference if no one has the software or downloaded application prior to the pandemic will add to the immediate chaos and convey a sense of the situation being out of control.

If you have clients that you have to meet with, consider using a good video online conference service that is easy to install and use. Your IT support, operational, managerial and sales staff can set-up the system on their computers prior to the outbreak, and conduct a trial run of the program free of charge, prior to having to meet for critical meetings during the peak infectivity. If you have to close your business for a short time, inform your clients in advance. Your clients will appreciate your thinking ahead and considering their welfare and business continuity. Developing a generic communication power point presentation for clients and/or employees before an event can save a lot of time and confusion when confronted by more pressing crisis-related issues.

Your communication plan should also include tools for management to communicate any decisions they make to staff to keep the business operating, if possible. Another key consideration that will need to be kept in mind involves investors and other financial stakeholders (such as banks), who should also be kept informed. By planning and protecting your business and communicating your plans and strategies, you will also communicate to your financial stakeholders that you are protecting their best interests.

The communications plan should carefully determine how to distribute passwords or other on-line protection tools for key internet functions to select personnel in advance. Scammers and other on-line hostiles will not take a vacation, and may seek to exploit a disruptive environment.

Continuity:

Consumer goods, parts and other goods coming out of Asia will be significantly impacted over the coming months. Already manufacturers, such as the Hyundai automobile plants in South Korea, have temporarily closed manufacturing operations because of a shortage of parts coming from China. If your business is reliant upon goods manufactured in China, South Korea, Japan and other Asian countries, plan ahead and stockpile what you can. It is reasonable to assume, even now, that things are only going to get worse before they get better.

Manufacturing on-demand means companies never have to warehouse inventory. Using immediate internet ordering, companies only manufacture the products that customers order. In a pandemic, that means there are no stockpiled parts waiting to be shipped. In the short term, rethink your ordering strategies to ensure continuity in your critical wholesale supply chains.

Cross training of personnel will provide another level of redundancy necessary to keep your business running smoothly during an outbreak. Think about what would happen if your key financial person suddenly was not available. Does your company have more than one person able to access financial records, pay bills and conduct banking? Does more than one person have access to key passwords? Your pandemic business plan should include plans for who has key information, such as passwords for banking, cloud services, internet and email conference administration, etc. The ability to conduct business through internet services, including check deposits, may be another item to consider. Brainstorm with key personnel to make sure that you have redundancy in all your financial and administrative systems, including internet-based systems. Remain flexible, focus on problem solving, and avoid blame or shame cycles. You will not be able to anticipate everything, and neither will your key managers and other critical employees.

Consider applying for a line of credit, finding new investors, arranging for an advance payroll loan and/or ensuring have your business has enough money on hand for coping with reduced production and/or services. Design a budget to specifically analyze and plan for your increased spending needs to get your business though the outbreak.

Safety plan:

Put a safety protection plan in place for the employees that must come into your physical locations, and develop a telecommuting work place plan for as many employees as possible.

The bio-threat is both employee-to-employee transmission of the virus as well as from customers and clients. Engineering controls may include providing masks, gloves and eye protection for workers or providing air purifiers in the workplace. Other examples might include erecting physical barriers between staff and customers or installing sneeze guards.

Administrative controls might include developing policies to cross train personnel, allow staff to work from home, and developing an internet/cloud-based system to provide customers and clients the ability to conduct business with your firm without having to be physically present.

Some business will have to make the tough decision to pay people off and let them go in advance. Keep this decision limited to a small number of personnel if possible, and delay implementation until the time comes. There is also a strong possibility that some workers will chose to quit once the outbreak gets underway. Both contingencies will require cross-training and re-assignment of other employees to new tasks, and will need to be considered.

Security:

If your business is retail or you have a physical location that you might have to close, there are things you can do to protect your business: Buy a good security camera system. The camera systems that are directly linked to your cell phone work very well and are not much money. Most have multiple cameras, as well as cameras that can be used indoors, outdoors and in low light situations.

If you have a retail business or keep valuables at the site, consider hiring a security firm to patrol the location. Store any valuables elsewhere and consider uploading important documents to a cloud based system. Consider having one employee or owner on site as much as possible, even if the business is closed. Infectious disease outbreaks can make otherwise sane and law-abiding people do crazy things.

Specialty business considerations:

The healthcare industry (physicians, physical therapists, dentists, etc.) and the food industry (such as restaurants, food delivery services and caterers) have many special considerations for closing or continuing business operations during a pandemic. Reach out to local health officials, business associations, and licensing organizations to help plan for these specialized business planning needs.

"In the Chinese language, the word 'crisis' is composed of two characters, one representing danger and the other, opportunity,"

(John F. Kennedy)

"Always smile, even if it's a sad smile, because sadder than a sad smile is the sadness of not being able to smile."
(Jim Morrison)

Chapter : 3
Important Terms to Know

Endemic

Adjective. (Of a condition or of a disease) prevalent or found regularly among a particular population, group or area.

When a disease is *endemic*, it means that it's commonplace amongst certain people, certain places, and in certain conditions. One would say that the common cold is *endemic* in

the wintertime. It's almost like you can expect people to come down with this particular illness when it's this time of year or when certain conditions are present.

"The bends are *endemic* amongst deep-sea divers and diving enthusiasts."

As of right now, coronavirus cannot be considered *endemic*. It is not nearly widespread enough for this and it's not as common as the news reports and viral media may have us believe. While it is a prevalent problem, it is far from reaching the *endemic* status that organizations such as the CDC or WHO would have to give it.

An illness that has become *endemic* are the ones that can predictably occur within a certain group, population, or in areas where specific conditions are typically present. One of the more well-known *endemic* illnesses in the United States is chicken pox. Most children who are young and in school, typically of about eight years of age or below, can be expected to contract and display symptoms of chicken pox. The disease is nearly always present in a given community, but in fairly low frequency.

In short, *endemic* illnesses and diseases are the ones that can be trusted to occur semi-frequently but are not a great cause for concern as we have figured out treatment for them and are quick to administer it when the time comes for us to do so. If your doctor has treatment or prevention options for such illnesses, such as vaccines and courses of medicinal treatment, it is best to follow their professional medical advice for the best possible results.

Epidemic

Noun. A prevalent spread of an infectious disease or illness within a community (large or small), striking many people and causing illness all at once.

Adjective. Having the nature or scope of an illness that is an epidemic.

Epidemic is probably the most commonly used word with the "-demic" suffix. This is the one that indicates a sudden, severe, and widespread of active cases of illness within a specific community or area. *Epidemics* can be on a small scale, like a school having several widespread cases throughout the different classrooms and grades.

The CDC says that an *epidemic* can occur when there are an adequate number of susceptible hosts and an adequate number of people carrying the illness in question are in a specific area. This allows the illness to branch out from the agent to those susceptible hosts and to take hold there. From there, the spread can continue in just the same way, causing a rash of cases in a short period of time, typically right inside the incubation period.

Being a susceptible host means that your immune system is either compromised or simply unacquainted with the illness enough to fight it off. The most common way for immune systems to get enough exposure to these illnesses in order to be able to fight them off when they encounter them is through vaccines.

A vaccine is a combination of the ***inactive*** strain of the illness and other things to help deliver that strain properly. When the inactive strain of the illness is properly introduced into your system, the antibodies and the immune system has a chance to identify the illness completely and break it down without too much issue in most cases. Once it's been able to fight off that illness once, the next time it encounters it in the active form, the immune system is equipped to handle it much more readily than it would otherwise be. This is why vaccinations are so important in society; to prevent previously eliminated illnesses from becoming a threat to public health once again.

Incubation period

Noun. The period of time between one's exposure to an illness or infection and the development or appearance of symptoms.

This is the period of time it takes from the moment of initial exposure for symptoms to develop. It's typically given in a range, as many illnesses can vary in the time they take to fully develop depending on many factors like your immune system health, where you are, the severity of the exposure, and some other factors.

When an illness enters the body, the warm temperatures and all the things inside the body can help to grow and feed the illness before it has the chance to be treated. In this time, it can multiply, it can change, it can get stronger, and it can even mutate. This is why it's so important that treatment be sought out as quickly as possible for illnesses that can't go away or be treated without medical care.

For COVID-19, the average incubation period is from two day to two weeks. You can still experience the onset of symptoms outside that range, but within that range is when it's most likely. If you notice that you spent some time with someone who was recently in a place that had a lot of patients with COVID-19 (even if they showed no symptoms) and a day later, you feel like you're coming down with something, seek medical attention immediately.

Some people are "carriers," which means they can give people the illness, but it hasn't taken hold in their system yet. There are no symptoms to identify carriers, so they're walking around spreading the illness with no idea that they're even doing it. This is why it's incredibly important to make sure that you are keeping yourself clean and healthy and that you're not touching things in a public space, then touching your face.

Outbreak

Noun. The occurrence of more cases than would normally be accepted in a particular area at that time.

Outbreak is the phrase that is typically used to call attention to a rash of illnesses without putting the label of "epidemic" on an illness. It still calls attention to the situation at hand, letting the public know that something could be wrong, but doesn't indicate that thousands of people are affected by the illness at one time.

Pandemic

Noun. An illness or disease that has become prevalent or widely affecting parts of an entire country, or the whole world.

Now, certain illnesses can be experienced all over the world. You are just as likely to get the flu in Canada as you are to get it in Poland, depending on the conditions and the medical care available. For an illness to be considered *pandemic,* all the cases that span across the country or across continents must be active simultaneously.

Some *pandemics* can be more severe than others, as some illnesses that have become *pandemic* are largely treatable, and the range of cases that constitutes a *pandemic* can be quite varied. Just make sure that, if you get wind that something is a *pandemic*, you look at the numbers before becoming too alarmed.

In addition to the raw numbers of how many cases, how many deaths, and how many recoveries, you look at the time it took for those numbers to rise. If it leaped up by 300 cases in a single day recently, you could say that there is cause for worry. However, if you found that the number of cases occurring is on the downswing (i.e. only ten cases in one day when previous days were in the hundreds), things are quickly being reeled back in.

Quarantine

Noun. This the state or period of being isolated or sequestered from the general population to allow an illness to take its course without spreading to others.

Verb. To place someone in such a state of isolation for such purposes.

You may have heard that many people are being quarantined, particularly in areas where there is a large outbreak. This is typically done to keep the illness from spreading to too many people in too short a time. You will generally see quarantines lasting for about two weeks.

By mitigating the spread of an illness, you can keep more people from getting sick and from missing out on the medical care they need in order to recover safely and quickly.

If you are placed in a quarantine, you will need to make provisions for yourself to keep yourself safely in your home for the duration of your quarantine. Some people are permitted to stay in their homes, while others are kept in a medical facility to ensure that if any care is needed during this time, access is fast and simple.

"In crises, a social epidemic breaks out that in any other era would have appeared to be a contradiction: the epidemic of overproduction."

(Karl Marx)

"The best way to overcome difficulties is to attack them with a magnificent smile."
(Robert Baden-Powell)

Chapter : 4
Who Is Most At Risk?

Everybody is suspectable of getting infected with the novel coronavirus, but elders and young children are at most risk. Because their bodies don't have a developed immune system they are at most risk, but it doesn't mean others aren't at risk. Those people are also at risk who have autoimmune problems and low immunity as compared to other healthy individuals.

On January 23, 2020, Chinese officials reported that people with prior health issues have the highest chances of death. On the other hand, women, children, and men who have no medical history have also perished at the hands of this virus.

More than 5 million people already left Wuhan even before the quarantine was placed on the city. So, there is a high chance of disease reaching other countries as well. Any American returning from China has to spend 14 days in quarantine before getting released and similar techniques are being used to monitor people coming from abroad, but some countries are not taking it seriously which could result in a sudden increase in the number of infected people and similarly one death has been reported outside of China in the Philippines.

The unfortunate guy was a 44-year-old Chinese who traveled from Wuhan to Hong Kong, and then to the Philippines. Officials say this is not a locally acquired case and the reported individual came from the epicenter of this outbreak. When reaching the Philippines he developed severe pneumonia and then died. The officials are also trying to track down the individuals on the same flight, the hotel staff who might have come into contact with him to quarantine them as well.

As of today, there are currently 24,628 cases world-wide with total deaths 492 and recovered are 911 people, the majority of people come from China. These numbers can fluctuate, but this the most accurate status of this epidemic at this time.

The risk factor is high as no vaccine is currently available to cure this disease, but we have positive news about the experimentation of different drugs and testing of a weak virus on different animals. But it is a long way before any mass produced vaccine will be available for the public.

What are the symptoms of the coronavirus?

The symptoms of the coronavirus are similar to that of other illnesses, and due to that, it has become very hard for authorities and doctors to monitor and diagnose the people with infection. Some symptoms such as fever are suppressible by taking drugs that help lowering fever, which makes it impossible for others to differentiate between normal and infected persons.

Coronaviruses commonly have a group of symptoms, but in rare cases, there can be severe symptoms that result in extreme effects on the patient's body. The incubation period for novel coronavirus ranges from 2 days to 14 days. This is based on previous incubation period knowledge about MERS. The precise incubation period for this virus is unknown, as it doesn't show any symptoms during this period. The invasion of the virus in the human body causes the following symptoms.

Pneumonia is the most common symptom of the Wuhan coronavirus because a large number of affected individuals experienced pneumonia. As this virus targets lung cells of humans for replication it results in the breakdown of lung tissue causing pneumonia.

Shortness of breath occurs due to poor gaseous exchange. As lungs are highly damaged during this viral infection, they are unable to absorb much oxygen according to body needs.

Extreme coughing is also experienced by people suffering from this virus as an automatic response of the human body to expel pathogens from our bodies. This cough is accompanied by sputum production or blood can also come in serious cases.

High fever is a major symptom of the coronavirus when the virus enters our body, it causes an increase in our body temperature, as an immune response to kill the incoming pathogens. Fever more than 100.4-degree Fahrenheit is observed in serious cases of the novel coronavirus.

Muscle pain is also a symptom of the coronavirus, as pain in the diaphragm due to extreme coughing is observed.

Runny nose and headaches are experienced by infected people as the virus produces flu-like symptoms in the initial stages.

In rare cases, kidney failure can also occur as the increased physical stress on the body causes the kidneys to lose their proper functioning of filtering the blood from waste and harmful materials.

Other body organs infected as a result of the infection spreading is called sepsis and is a symptom in severe cases of the coronavirus.

Due to extreme physical deterioration, this viral infection can lead to patients passing out caused by a lack of fluids and an improper supply of oxygen.

A person experiencing some of these symptoms should be hospitalized, as there are a lot of chances that he is suffering from novel coronavirus, lack of data refrains us from getting to know about how lethal this virus is. Residents of Wuhan believe that the official tally of people infected with coronavirus is much lower than the actual number because many people with flu-like symptoms are not attended to due to an increased number of patients in hospitals and a shortage of testing kits.

Severe symptoms are observed in people who are aged because of their weakened immune system. Their immune system is not able to cope with the viral load, and it results in death. Smokers are affected increasingly because their lung cells are already damaged due to smoking. So, when a virus attacks them, they are not able to develop immunity. Infants also have an underdeveloped immune system that places them at an increased risk of getting infected by this virus.

"The fascination of history and its enigmatic lesson is that, from age to age, nothing changes and yet everything is completely different."

   (Aldous Huxley)

"Heaven has given three things to men to compensate for life's difficulties: hope, sleep and a smile."

   (Immanuel Kant)

Chapter : 5
Modern Virus

What is the coronavirus?

One of the most potentially damaging comments that keeps being posted to social media is that "the coronavirus is just the common cold." This statement comes from a misunderstanding of what a coronavirus actually is (and what it isn't).

The term coronavirus isn't a catchall. Instead, it describes a family of viruses that have crown-like spikes when viewed through a medical microscope. According to the Centers for Disease Control and Prevention (CDC), coronaviruses first came to our attention in the 1960s. Since then, seven distinct coronaviruses with the ability to infect humans have been identified.

The first four are common and aren't typically very serious. They include:

- 229E (alpha coronavirus)
- OC43 (beta coronavirus)
- NL63 (alpha coronavirus)
- HKU1 (beta coronavirus)

Within these first four coronaviruses are some of the viruses that cause the common cold. It's important to note that a cold can also be caused by viruses that are not part of the coronavirus family.

Next, we have three coronaviruses that have the potential to cause great harm to humans.

- MERS-CoV (beta coronavirus, 858 fatalities)
- SARS-CoV (beta coronavirus, 774 fatalities)
- COVID-19/SARS-CoV-2* (unknown, Wuhan Coronavirus, 3,828 reported fatalities from December 31, 2019 – March 8, 2020)

*NOTE: Renamed from 2019-nCoV to 2019-nCoV ARD on January 30, then renamed again on February 11 to COVID-19 [the disease] and SARS-CoV-2 [the virus].

MERS (Middle East Respiratory Syndrome) sickened at least 2,494 people. The mortality rate of this illness was very high, with approximately 34 percent of the infected passing away from MERS.

SARS (Severe Acute Respiratory Syndrome) sickened at least 8,098 people. The mortality rate of this illness was much lower than MERS at approximately 9.5 percent.

As of March 8, 2020, there were 110,007 reported COVID-19 (Coronavirus Disease 2019) infections. Of those, at least 3,828 died. This indicated an expected fatality rate of 3.4 percent, which was publicly stated by the World Health Organization on March 4, 2020.

To put this into context, the flu's mortality rate during an average season is approximately 0.01-0.02 percent. Of course, 42.9 million Americans got the flu in the 2018-2019 season, so even a mortality rate of 0.01 percent led to 61,200 deaths.

By comparison, the 1918 Spanish Flu pandemic claimed the lives of an estimated 3-6 percent of all infected individuals. Because the Spanish Flu grew to a global infection rate of around 500 million people and claimed more lives in some nations than others, it's believed that at least 50 million people died during the pandemic.

It is still unlikely that the 2019 novel coronavirus (Wuhan) will spread to hundreds of millions of people worldwide, although this could change as the virus continues to spread. If it did infect that many people, the death total would almost certainly be in the tens of millions.

According to a scientific assessment released on January 27, 2020, the expected number of infections was approximately 59,000 with 1,500 fatalities. This assumed a successful quarantine rate of 90 percent of global cases. Scientific modeling predicted a much more dire situation with a quarantine rate below 90 percent. In the unlikely instance of only a 50 percent quarantine rate, the number of infected people could rise as high as 5 million, with more than 100,000 fatalities.

By March 8, the infections had already surpassed the expected number by more than 51,000, and the deaths had more than doubled the initial projection. This seems to suggest that the quarantine rate fell beneath 90 percent, but there's no way to verify what the rate actually was or if it was still dropping.

The more likely scenario was originally predicted to closely mirror SARS and MERS, putting fatalities at or below 1,500. However, it is crucial to note that 5 million people made it out of the Wuhan area before the quarantine zone was enacted, which likely made a big difference in COVID-19's global growth.

It's impossible to know how many cases and fatalities will eventually be confirmed or how far the virus will spread. As of March 8, 3,828 people had already perished, and the virus had been found in more than 100 countries/territories across six continents.

What are the symptoms?

The three most common symptoms of coronavirus are:

- Coughing

- Fever

- Shortness of breath

The symptoms of COVID-19 have been known to appear between two and fourteen days of being exposed to the illness. If you've been around someone with the illness within the last two weeks and you start to notice symptoms, you should call your doctor immediately.

Many people have reported the feelings of coronavirus ranging from mild to flu-like, to quite severe. If you feel like you're coming down with this illness, prepare yourself to go outdoors by using an appropriate face mask that will prevent the spread of illness, and call ahead to let your doctor know you're coming. Let them know what you think you might be dealing with and what your most recent exposure was like, and see if there are any special accommodations they need to make before allowing you into their office to be near other patients. By making the medical professionals aware of the possibility of an illness, we help to mitigate its spread and we help to keep it from getting out of hand.

If you have shortness of breath and you are unsure of your ability to breathe during travel, talk with your doctor about what options might be available to you for transport, or consider calling an ambulance to safely get you into the care of medical professionals. When calling for EMT transport, specify what you believe your situation to be so the EMTs can take proper preventive measures to keep any illness from spreading to them or to the other patients they help throughout the rest of their shift.

How does the virus spread?

The virus is mainly spread from person to person, meaning that it's not airborne and that you won't come down with it by drinking from the municipal water supply. The best ways to keep yourself from contracting this illness is to limit your contact with people who are or may be infected. Let's take a look at some specifics:

Try to keep about six feet between you and other people that you don't know. For many people who take public transportation, this is quite tricky. When you're in public, you want to try to keep a bubble around you of about six feet. If you feel like you aren't able to keep that distance, then do your best to sanitize yourself frequently and wear a mask that will help you to keep yourself from breathing in any contaminants between sanitizing.

Try to keep from breathing in the air near where someone coughed or sneezed. The little droplets left behind in the air when someone coughs or sneezes are a prime way for the illness to spread. If someone is in close quarters with you and coughs or sneezes, do your best to keep clear of the area or make sure that you have your mask on your face. In such cases that prohibit you from exiting the area, using a disinfectant spray can be helpful to neutralize any droplets or contaminants in the air, making it safe to walk through that area once again. Ensure that you don't spray any such disinfectants onto anyone who may be standing nearby, as this could cause skin irritation.

If you happen to be a little too close when someone sneezes or coughs, it's possible to breathe it in. This is a most unpleasant situation to even imagine, but if you happen to be in a space when someone coughs or sneezes a little too close to you and you either get it in your mouth or breathe it in, you need to act quickly. If it's in your mouth, try to use a germ- killing mouth wash and do not swallow any saliva until the area has been sanitized. Wash your face with soap and warm water, and make sure to get any residual matter wiped away and the areas sanitized. Wash your hands regularly.

What is the incubation period?

The incubation period is typically between two days and two weeks. It is possible for symptoms to manifest outside of these times, but this is the most typical for the cases that have been established.

At the time of writing, there are about 82,550 cases of coronavirus worldwide and 33,243 of those cases have fully recovered. This might seem low when you look at the raw numbers, but what it's important to know is that of the

~49,000 cases that are not yet marked as recovered, only 2,810 of those have succumbed to the illness, giving it a much lower mortality percentage than influenza.

If you have been around people who have coronavirus, or if you have been in an area with a high concentration of cases, keep an eye on yourself for about two weeks for the onset of symptoms. If you start to cough, feel feverish, feel shortness of breath, or if you notice flu symptoms, it is best to make an appointment to talk with your doctor about the possibility of treatment for coronavirus.

What should I do if I think I have it?

Call your doctor immediately. If you have good reason to suspect that you have contracted the illness from others who have or are carrying the illness, then you should get in contact with your doctor to seek out your next steps. In many cases, they will direct you to a hospital or a treatment center, though they may prefer to see you and offer an alternative diagnosis before you turn to other, more drastic routes of treatment.

With all the attention that this illness is getting right now, there are a lot of cases in which the patient is utterly convinced they have come down with coronavirus, only to find out that they simply have the common cold or allergies thanks to the changing of the weather.

In the February-March period of the year, the environment around you may be changing from winter to spring. This means that plants all around you are coming back into bloom, there is pollen everywhere, and there is a high concentration of allergens swimming about outside. This can cause severe allergy flare-ups in people that seem quite severe. Because allergies also cause coughing and shortness of breath, you will want to be certain this isn't what's going on with you before you seek treatment in a center with real cases of coronavirus.

It's bad enough to think you have a serious disease, only to find out you're just having an allergy attack. Let's not add the injury to insult by actually giving you the chance to contract the illness from bona fide patients!

If you think you might be coming down with coronavirus, speak with your doctor, wash your hands, don't share meals or cups with others, limit your contact with others, and await instruction from the professionals!

"There can't be a crisis next week. My schedule is already full."

(Henry Kissinger)

"In our chest we carry colonies of butterflies that are waiting for the happy moment when we laugh to soar into the air."
(Fabrizio Caramagna)

Chapter : 6
The World's Response the Coronavirus

Health organizations response – what are the WHO, CDC and ECDC doing?

The World Health Organization (WHO) has been with the coronavirus since the first day it was made public. In fact, it was the WHO office in China who first officially raised the alarm in the international community. The WHO has also published a large amount of educative content meant to teach the world about preventing coronavirus infections. Additionally, they are tracking and measuring all parameters of the situation and issuing guidance whenever necessary. The main goal of the organization is to build preparedness, raise awareness, take steps in emergencies as well as coordinate and direct the effort to contain and eradicate the virus.

On the other hand, it's the job of the Center for Disease Control (CDC) to work on solving the problem directly. At the moment of writing, the CDC is taking the following actions:

- Preparing first responders, medical facilities and healthcare professionals to deal with the current scale of the coronavirus outbreak as well as any potential future development.
- The CDC has published 23 different guidance documents to instruct people on the best courses of action for their specific circumstances.
- Utilizing and promoting telehealth tools to minimize the risk of spreading infection.
- Analyzing and assisting in correcting any detected errors in current healthcare systems in regard to dealing with the coronavirus outbreak.
- Creating links between medical facilities and professionals to improve integration, increase direct communication and ease logistical aspects of the outbreak management.
- Various other preventive and educative measures.

The CDC created the test for coronavirus and they are working on a viable serology test as well. The development of a test for this virus was done exceptionally quickly and was a powerful demonstration of the CDC's resolve, efficiency and professionalism.

Meanwhile, the European Center for Disease Control (ECDC) is trying to keep the situation under control in Europe and especially Italy. At the moment, community spreading is in full swing in Italy and further measures are being considered.

Government responses

Chinese reaction

As the coronavirus started on their territory, the Chinese government was been quick to implement prevention and health security measures to protect their vast population. International observers and medical professionals who were involved with the SARS outbreak of 2003 noted that the Chinese cooperated far better in this outbreak, and they did a far better job of managing it than last time. Even so, the Chinese did attempt to cover the infection up in the beginning, but due to the highly infectious nature of the virus, more stringent measures were required and they quickly started cooperating.

As a result of the need for more restrictions, the Chinese government quarantined the city of Wuhan and several other cities and provinces implemented their own security measures. Following these actions, new infection rates started to drop almost immediately, while recovery rates started to grow and have been growing continuously ever since.

In a bid to garner international support but also to prevent future outbreaks such as the animal-derived coronavirus, the Chinese government has introduced a permanent ban on consuming, buying or selling any type of wild animal specifically used for food. However, this still doesn't apply to wild animals (dead or alive) bought for medicinal purposes.

International community reactions

For once, it seems that the entire international community is standing together, united amongst each other, as well as with the scientific and medical communities to find a vaccine, cure or any type of solution for the coronavirus outbreak. Governments all over the world are cooperating through the official channels and even a single confirmed case in any given country will get the proper attention, especially if that country is not financially ready to treat large numbers of infected patients.

The president of the United States, Donald J. Trump created a special task force to help fight the spread of coronavirus in the country, putting his vice-president Mike Pence in charge of the job. Additionally, the US has introduced scans and screenings at all entry points of the country, including all international airports.

The Italian government has effectively quarantined around 100,000 people by instituting lockdowns and security measures in north Italy, the region which was hardest hit by the coronavirus outbreak. Both Italy and France have shut down cultural institutions and either postponed or cancelled planned events where crowds could help the virus spread quickly.

Evacuations

Immediately after the outbreak, nations started evacuating their citizens from countries with an increased risk of infection. The United States began to evacuate their citizens from Wuhan on January 28th, with the EU, Australia, India, New Zealand and others quickly following their example. Also, multiple countries have evacuated their citizens from Iran, Italy, South Korea and Japan. Yes, these are the countries with the largest numbers of citizens infected with the coronavirus, but also countries where the virus is spreading through the community. The latter is the defining factor in the international decision to remove their citizens as soon as possible. As the virus strikes the United States, we will no doubt see other countries evacuate their own citizens from the Land of the Free.

International aid

International aid organizations such as Direct Relief and various other NGOs have already established bases of operation in heavily affected areas. Also, some countries have started to send medical equipment and material to China, Iran and Italy.

Donated equipment usually includes protective suits, face masks including N95s, medical gloves and other protective gear, but it's not uncommon to find all sorts of donations. The idea behind these international donations is that we can stop the spreading of the virus in infected areas if protective equipment is issued not only to medical professionals, but also to the general public, thereby limiting the virus' potential to spread unimpeded through the community.

The situation is still ongoing and I'm sure this will all seem like old news in a month, but at the time, it's very important to note that the world is actually trying to come together on this issue.

But, as we all know, money makes the world turn. So, how did the business community react to the outbreak?

Business community response

The business community warned the world that the situation with the coronavirus would be bad for the economy a couple of days after an outbreak was confirmed. Ever since then, there have been increasingly pessimistic predictions for the future of international commerce, as well as the possibility of a recession following the containment of the disease.

China is the world's biggest supplier of goods and makes up 14% of the world's economy. So, it can't be good that over 300 million people have been sent home or quarantined. Businesses in the affected areas in China have either been working at a reduced capacity or have closed entirely, which means the Chinese economy is going to be suffering until the outbreak ends.

On the world markets, the S&P 500 dropped by 11.5% - its largest drop since the financial disaster of 2008. As the situation develops, the business community is yet to provide a solid response to the coronavirus threat.

Sports organizations response

As the panic over the coronavirus outbreak goes global, numerous crowded events are cancelled to contain the spread. Italy has postponed a large number of soccer games and ordered most of the games played in the northern part of the country to be played without spectators. Switzerland suspended its soccer league entirely, Chinese soccer has been postponed, as has the Asian Champions League. Additionally, events have been either postponed or cancelled in tennis, golf, indoor track and field, racing and moto racing, rugby and cycling. The Tokyo marathon was also conducted without spectators and with only a few hundred selected runners – just like the biathlon World Cup in the Czech Republic. More sporting events are being cancelled by the minute as the world fears the threat of the coronavirus.

But, as the world gets its information from media and social media, let's talk about how these organizations and tools have responded to humanity's latest disaster.

Media & social media

"Infodemic."

That is the word used by the World Health Organization in reference to the flurry of information regarding the coronavirus all over media and social media. Millions of people around the world have been misinformed about various aspects of this disease, but legitimate media outlets and health-conscious individuals and organizations are actively trying to combat stories with facts.

Traffic redirection is just one of the measures undertaken by the WHO, in partnership with social media websites such as Facebook, Twitter and Instagram. This means that when people get online and search for "coronavirus", they are redirected to the websites of the CDC, WHO or their local health ministry, depending on their location. The WHO is also creating informational content in a large number of languages to combat misinformation.

For the entire duration of the outbreak, media teams from all over the world have tried to cover the coronavirus outbreak as meticulously as possible in order to present a fact-checked version of the events to the wary general public. The largest and most-visited websites have live updates minute-by- minute, while smaller news outlets regularly cover the coronavirus outbreak in their programs.

Meanwhile, on social media, users are sharing pretty much everything. Like always, the situation has partially turned to humor expressed in memes and viral trends (in true social media fashion — pun intended!) such as the Wuhan shake and the Vietnamese anti-coronavirus song. Of course, users are also sharing valuable information and facts about the virus, but they are swimming in a sea of misinformation, fake news, obvious lies and made-up stories as well as malicious content.

To help fight the infodemic, several social media sites have responded with their own measures. For example, Facebook now removes all posts about fake cures and treatments posted on its platform – and we all know how much clutter this creates. Moreover, Facebook fact-checks posted articles to make sure they're not fake news and it lets the user know when they click on it. Another one of their measures was the removal of ads for face masks, claiming to be the "very last available masks".

International politics spilled over into social media as well, with Russia being accused of using the coronavirus panic to spread misinformation and conspiracy theories about the United States on social media.

As everything else on these platforms, this too will blow over fairly quickly and we will draw our conclusions and learn lessons once the infodemic is over.

But until then, the major point of constriction for the world being caused by the coronavirus outbreak – is travel.

"Moments of crisis double the vitality in men. Or perhaps, more in money: men only begin to live fully when their backs are against the wall."

(Paul Auster)

"It was only a smile, and it cost little to give it but, like the morning light, it dispelled the darkness and made the day worth   living."

(F. Scott Fitzgerald)

Chapter: 7
Social, Economic, and Political Impact of the Coronavirus

Social impact

As with any other global outbreak, the coronavirus has a strong effect on the social order of our world, and while some people are acting counterproductively by sharing incorrect information, for others this outbreak has been an opportunity to band together. Social media is once again proving to be a common ground for the vast majority of people – a place where they can educate each other on correctly enforced protection measures and prevention.

The CDC's instructions on planning for the coronavirus' arrival in your community outline the importance of positive and active communication between friends, neighbors and coworkers as a preventive measure. People are being brought together out of concern and they must stay united until the outbreak is contained.

Economic impact

The economic impact of the coronavirus outbreak has been huge and will continue to grow to even larger proportions as the virus spreads all over the planet. The full effect will be known once the outbreak is over and will depend on the timing of the discovery of the vaccine or cure, the overall effect on global health and population and the rigorousness as well as effectiveness of prevention and control measures.

There are some estimates that businesses producing over 70% of China's GDP have been closed, dealing an economic hit to the country. Furthermore, the Chinese are the biggest spenders in tourism, which has seen a steep and heavy decline after the outbreak. As China drives the growth of the global economy forward, depending on the severity of the outbreak in the future, it may bring financial consequences for the entire world by reducing everyone else's financial growth along their own.

The G20 and the IMF are already analyzing the possible aftermath of the coronavirus outbreak and will present their findings when they're ready. For now, the IMF has said that they don't expect any long-term negative economic effects after the outbreak, but they've also said that the longer this virus persists and spreads, the more it will inexorably impact the global economy in unforeseeable negative ways.

Political impact

Last time China had an outbreak similar to this one, they didn't want foreign organizations and governments meddling in their methods and questioning their actions. In the meantime, however, China became an even larger part of the world economy and that prompted changes in their system as well. Differing from the SARS outbreak in 2003, the Chinese government has been extensively praised for their cooperation with foreign organizations and governments during the outbreak of COVID-19. They have provided data transparency and even allowed criticism of local officials – something highly unusual for this country.

The coronavirus also became a topic for discussion in the democratic candidate election campaigns in the United States. Unlike most topics, this one was not a point of division among the candidates – each of them criticized the Trump administration over its handling of the outbreak and its delayed reactions to international developments.

These reactions are not unexpected, as previously President Trump expressed his opinion that the April heat would kill the virus and the entire thing would blow over, which is not only scientifically incorrect, but puts the lives of American people at risk through misinformation. In the aftermath of the democratic debates, the candidates have repeatedly promised that any future US administration would actually believe in science and hold to scientific principles.

Nevertheless, there are probably thousands of instances of chances in the political order caused by the COVID-19 outbreak. We are chronologically too close to the events and not enough time has passed for us to be able to determine the exact ramifications and political consequences of the outbreak.

The future will tell

For now, the questions of political, social and economic impact of the coronavirus outbreak will go only partially answered and the best anyone without a time machine can do is guess.

Hindsight is 20/20, and people reading this book a decade from now will know the correct answer to the question – "what mark did the coronavirus leave on human civilization?"

The world after the coronavirus

The world after the coronavirus outbreak is reserved for future generations, but we decide what type of world we are going to leave behind.

Humanity has had more than its fair share of epidemics and pandemics – and we've survived all of them so far.

We've been killed by viruses and bacteria in the tens of millions and we've survived.

We've even had our numbers reduced by double-digit percentages and we still made it.

The coronavirus is nothing new to us as a species and we will survive it just as we did every other one in the past – either by curing all current infected patients, vaccinating the healthy general population or treating patients in the conventional way.

But the trouble with the COVID-19 isn't that we don't have a vaccine yet, it's that while it has a lower fatality rate than its predecessors, it is far more infective and transmits more easily from person to person. This causes the number of infected to skyrocket, and even with a 3% fatality rate there will be thousands, if not tens of thousands of deaths. There have already been over 3,000 deaths, which is more than three times the number of people killed by SARS, in a quarter of the time!

We determine the future of our world and the legacy of coronavirus.

We get to choose.

A terrible disease dominating our public discourse in the following years?

Or do we follow scientific and medical procedures and stop it in its tracks now just to watch it fizzle away from public memory, only to be used as a reference to future events?

As a human being, my choice is no choice at all — we will defeat the coronavirus.

We must.

"The fact that men do not learn much from history is the most important lesson history teaches us."

(Aldous Huxley)

"A smile is like a toothbrush. You have to use it often to keep your teeth clean."

(Japanese proverb)

Chapter : 8
Protecting Yourself Using Mask

One method used to deter disease transmission is face masks. These can also be called dental masks, separation masks, layer masks, surgical masks, surgery masks. There's a lot of new brands come in different colors. The usage of an FDA approved face mask is critical. Facemasks tend to reduce germ dissemination. They emit tiny drops into the air when someone speaks, coughs, or sneezes that can affect others. When someone becomes infected a face mask will limit the number of germs produced by the wearer and can prevent people from being sick. Often, a facial mask covers the wearer's nose and mouth from body fluid splashes or sprays.

How to place the mask on

1. To remove the air particles, choose an N95 cap. This is a safe choice for shielding the lungs from air pollutants, which can be metal fumes (such as those created by welding), crystals, and dust or biological spores, such as viruses. You should use one if a flu outbreak has arisen in your area, or if pollution or fire have caused poor air quality. Such masks are made of lightweight and organized foam, which fit over the nose and

    mouth. • Models made particularly for people with manufacturing work and medical models for health care workers are also available. • The sum corresponds to the proportion of particles filterable by the cap. The N95 mask filters dust and contaminants at 95 percent.

    • If oil aerosols are available, these masks will not be used because the oil affects the filter. The "N" means "not immune to crude."

2. When you are exposed to a sticky environment, opt for the R or P mask. Search for a mask marked R or P in situations where the skin is exposed to natural, insect, vegetable or synthetic oils; The "R" means "slightly oil immune," meaning you would be shielded from oil vapors for a time limit specified on the package. • Such masks also come with numerical classifications such as P100 and R95. "P" means "oil proof or very resistant."

The numbers reflect the percentage of the filtered particles.
• When you are exposed to gasses or vapors that are more toxic than these masks ' concentration levels, opt for a respirator that uses filters or tubes to clean the air more efficiently.

3. To achieve the best match seek various sizes. The available sizes are additionally mini, mini, medium and large, depending on the specific N95 mask you select. Check for a few styles before making the order, if possible. Make sure the mask fits secure and doesn't fall off of your nose, knowing you're always trying to mold it to your nose and it's best suited. If you're unsure, pick a smaller size to ensure it doesn't spill out.

4. If you have some respiratory or heart disease, see a doctor. N95 masks will make breathing more difficult, particularly if you're got a chronic heart or respiratory condition. Speak to a doctor for more steps that you should take. You may be able to use an exhalation valve model that can facilitate respiration and reduce heat retention within the mask, but such models cannot be used if you intend to preserve a clean area, such as
an operating room. Speak to the doctor before you use it if you have any of the following disorders: • respiratory difficulties • emphysema • chronic

obstructive pulmonary disease (COPD) •asthma •
cardiac failure

5. Purchase an Amazon or retail store N95 mask
   approved by the NIOSH. In the hardware stores or home
   improvement shops, and in pharmacies, you can buy an N95
   cap. You can order it from internet retailers, including 3 M,
   directly too. It's necessary to buy only masks approved by
   the National Institute for Occupational Health and Safety
   (NIOSH). Such masks should have the NIOSH mark on the
   box of the same thing, as well as a qualification
   identification number.

   • When an N95 mask is required for work, the
   employer will generally supply it. • Masks which are
   not NIOSH- certified may not grant adequate
   protection.

6. Stock up on masks and that you need them you are set. They
   continue to be in high demand and sell quickly at such
   periods, such as during an infectious disease epidemic or
   when an area is suffering extreme pollution. Stay ready to
   still get plenty at your side for you and your family
   members. Seek to get 2 or 3 masks per member of your
   family, so they're healthy.

• Taking the local climate into account when providing
  masks. For example, if you live in a big city with

significant pollution issues, you'll need more than if you live in a healthier, more rural environment.

7   Before using the mask, remove your facial hair where possible. When you know you need to wear an N95 mask, then shave the hair on your forehead. This can be a mask barrier and avoid airtight closing, which will reduce its performance. When there is an emergency situation and you don't have time to shave, put as many as you can on the suit.

8   Wash your hands before putting your mask on. Using soap and rinse, and then wipe your hands so it won't get dirty. This measure will keep you from contaminating it by mistake until it is placed on.

9   Take the mask in one hand and place it over the nose and lips. Place it on the hand side, with the stripes facing the wall. Place it on the nose and mouth and attach the nose guard on the nose bridge. The edge of the lip will go down. To keep it safe, just try to touch the outside and the sides of the mask.

10 Pull the strips upper and lower over the ear. If the mask has two bands, put the bottom one over the head and tie it under the mouth, around the throat. With the other hand keeps the mask tightly to the nose. Then take the top strip and put it over the ears. Fix the top side of the mask. The mask side with a rigid bendable

edge is the top and is designed to conform to the shape of the nose.

Determine which hand is at the front of the mask. Typically the front is the colored side of the mask, which will face away from you, while the white side covers your nose.

11 Forms the nose shield along the nose bridge. Place the first two fingers on the top of the mask on either side of the nasal metal film. Race all sides of the strip with your fingertips, shaping it over the nose bridge. • If there is no nasal shield in the suit, just make sure it's snug around the nose.

12 Search at alternative options at youth. The N95 masks aren't made for kids and they won't suit well. If the air quality is poor, bring as many of the children as possible indoors. Take extra precautions in the case of flu outbreaks (such as helping children wash their hands before meals and after sneezing or coughing). You should even try purchasing specially made masks for kids, even though they aren't N95. Don't wear an N95 mask on children under the age of 17 or 18.

An older teenager can wear an N95 mask to check for fit and comfort. If the mask suits properly and provides a strong barrier, ask him to continue and walk around and look out for

any sense of vertigo or breathing difficulties. Ask him to delete
it if such signs occur, and go inside.

13 Breathe by the mask and search for leaks. Place your hands
on the mask and take a breath to make sure the face shuts.
Then exhale to see if there is any leaking inside or along the
edges of the nasal guard. When you feel the air rushing
through the region of your nose, reshape the nasal protector.
When it appears from the

top, change the strips on the sides of the eyes. • If the
mask is not yet completely removed, ask your buddy or
relative to help you, or seek another size or pattern.

14 Replace the mask by drawing the lines over the head
rim. Pull the bottom strip over the eyes, without reaching
the front of the mask. Let it hang up over the chest. Instead,
put the strip on top. • Its either you throw the mask
away or put it in a jar or in a clean, sealed bag.

15 Give away the mask if you have used it in a medical
environment. If you used it on a sick patient or as a means
to stop being ill during an epidemic, it's definitely infected
the ground. Proper handling of it should guarantee you do
not come into contact with infected materials. Carefully
keep the strip mask and dump it into a garbage bin.

16 Use the mask again as long as it stays dry and suits snugly. When you use it to protect yourself from environmental threats and have not come into contact with dangerous germs, you will not be having trouble using it again. Seek to remove the mask while you wear it, to make sure it suits properly. Place in a jar or in a clean, closed bag, and make sure the nearby items will not distort it.

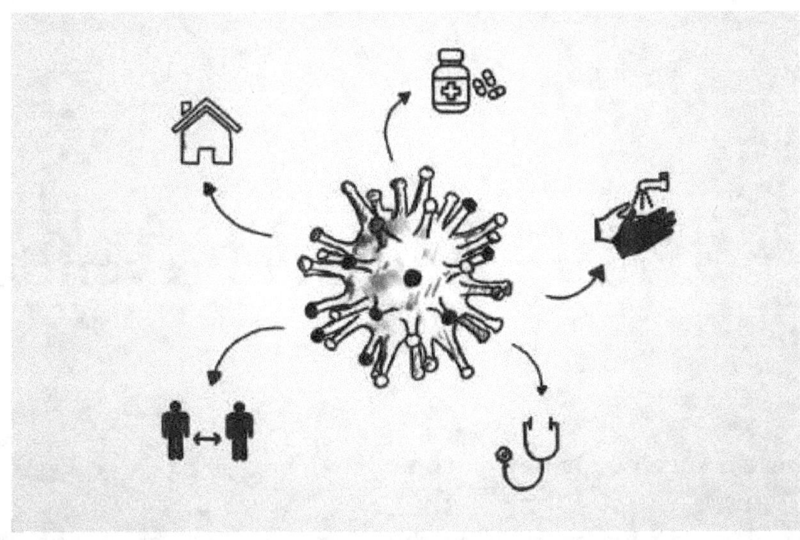

"If medicines now cure the disease, but not the sick person, there must be a medicine in the future that will cure only the sick person and not the disease".

(Hernán Huarache Mamani)

"A delicate word, a kind look, a good-natured smile can shape wonders and perform miracles."
(William Hazlitt)

Chapter: 9
Treatments and Prevention

Is there a vaccine for new coronavirus?

No, since it is another sickness, there is no vaccine yet and the time required to cause one to can be generally long (it is evaluated 12-18 months).

What would I be able to do to secure myself?

Keep yourself educated about the spread of the plague, accessible on the WHO site and take the accompanying individual safeguard measures:

- Wash your hands regularly with cleanser and water or alcohol-based solutions for expelling the virus from your hands.

- Keep a specific separation - at any rate, two meters - from others, particularly when they hack or sneeze or in the event that they have a fever, in light of the fact that the infection is contained in salivation beads and can be transmitted by breathing at short proximity

- Abstain from contacting your eyes, nose and mouth with your hands on the off chance that you have a fever, hack or trouble breathing and have as of late made a trip to China or in the event that you have been in close contact with an individual who has come back from China and has respiratory malady.

- Recollect that there are a few reasons for respiratory sickness and the new coronavirus might be one of them. On the off chance that you have gentle side effects and have not been to contaminated regions, remain at home until the side effects are settled by applying cleanliness measures, which incorporate hand cleanliness (wash your hands regularly with cleanser and water or liquor arrangements) and aviation route cleanliness (sniffle or hack in a cloth or with your elbow flexed, utilize a cover and toss the pre- owned tissues in a shut bushel following use and wash your hands).

Is the virus transmitted by food?

Regularly respiratory maladies are not transmitted through food, however, they should be taken care of regarding great cleanliness rehearses and staying away from contact among crude and prepared food.

Do I need to wear a mask to secure myself?

The World Health Organization suggests wearing a mask just on the off chance that you presume that you have gotten the new Coronavirus and have indications, for example, hacking or sneezing or on the off chance that you are dealing with an individual with suspected new Coronavirus contamination. The utilization of the veil assists with restricting the spread of the infection yet ought to be taken notwithstanding other respiratory and hand cleanliness measures. It isn't helpful to wear a few covers on one another. The normal utilization of veils is imperative to maintain a strategic distance from superfluous misuse of significant assets.

Masks or Respirators?

Before we go any further, let's simply explain on a specialized contrast between a "mask" and a "mask with respirator". In everyday language, we frequently state masks, when alluding to what is in fact called respirators.

Uses of simple Masks:

- Masks are baggy, covering the nose and mouth
- Designed for one path security, to catch natural liquid leaving the wearer
- Example – worn during medical procedure to forestall hacking, sniffling and so on the exposed patient
- Contrary to conviction, masks DO NOT secure the wearer
- The greater part of covers don't have a security rating relegated to them (for example NIOSH or EN)

Uses of Mask with Respirators:

- Respirators are tight-fitting covers, intended to make a facial seal
- Designed for two-path security, by sifting the air took in
- These DO secure the wearer (when worn appropriately), up to the wellbeing rating of the cover
- Available as a dispensable, half face or full face

What kinds of masks are useful?

While surgical style masks are not excess using any and all means, they're not perfect on account of an exceptionally transmissible airborne infection, since they don't sift through little particles, for example, viruses. To do this we need a respirator with a satisfactory safety rating.

The US Center for Disease Control (CDC) refers to the N95 respirator standard as a feature of the prompted defensive tool in their Covid-19 FAQ and their SARS direction (SARS being a comparable kind of Corona infection). Which proposes that N95 or better is adequate.

Are N95/N100 superior to FFP2/FFP3?

All things considered, no. It's essential to take note that these measures just indicate the base % of particles that the respirator channels. For instance, if a cover is FFP2 evaluated, it will channel in any event 94% of particles that are 0.3 microns in diameter or larger. Yet, by and by it will channel somewhere close to 94% and 99%. The exact figure will frequently be cited by the producer in the item portrayal.

Another genuine model is the GVS Ellipse respirator, which in the USA is appraised at P100 and in Europe is evaluated at P3, however, it is indicated to 99.97% for USA and 99.95% for Europe.

How enormous is COVID-19 and would respirators be able to channel it?

An ongoing paper shows that COVID-19 territories from somewhere in the range of 0.06 and 0.14 microns in size. Respirator's are estimated by their proficiency at separating particles of 0.3 microns and greater (and COVID-19 is littler than that).

This doesn't anyway imply that respirators can't channel littler particles.

Paddy Robertson has composed an extraordinary article regarding this matter, referring to look into indicating that the respirators tried could channel down to 0.007 microns (a lot littler than COVID-19). For instance, the 3M 8812 respirator (FFP1 evaluated) had the option to channel 96.6% of particles

> microns or bigger. Proposing FFP2 or FFP3 would accomplish considerably more prominent filtration.

Furthermore, this distribution by 3M talks about research demonstrating that N95 veils can proficiently channel as low as 0.05 microns.

Is Eye Protection Necessary?

While the coronavirus can't enter skin, it can infiltrate all uncovered mucous layers, which incorporates the eyes.

This is the reason you regularly observe clinical experts wearing eye veils when in contact with contaminated patients.

So, eyes are probably a lower chance as a course of passage, contrasted with the mouth, which is continually breathing air straightforwardly into the lungs.

How would I put on and remove the mask?

Here is the manner by which to do it:

- Prior to putting on the veil, wash your hands with cleanser and water or ethanol solution.
- Cover the mouth and nose with the veil guaranteeing that it is unblemished and clings well to the face
- Abstain from contacting the mask while wearing it, on the off chance that you contact it, wash your hands
- At the point when it gets wet, supplant it with another one and don't reuse it; as dispensable covers
- Evacuate the cover by taking it from the versatile and don't contact the front of the veil; quickly toss it into a shut sack and wash your hands.

Is there a treatment for new coronavirus?

There is no particular treatment for the illness brought about by new coronavirus. Treatment must be founded on the patient's manifestations. Steady treatment can be viable. Explicit treatments are being examined.

Would antibiotics be able to be valuable to forestall contamination with new coronavirus?

No, anti-microbials are not compelling against viruses, however, just neutralize bacterial contaminations.

What else would you be able to do?

- Normal hand washing/sterilizing
- Especially after you've been out and before eating.
- Sterilize your mobile phone
- Given how regularly we utilize our telephones, this appears the following intelligent need to be disinfected. Utilizing antibacterial wipes to clean your telephone and different things is a decent choice. Search for wipes that guarantee to have the option to do away with the flu virus (H1N1) − as that is a decent sign they might have the option to do comparative for the coronavirus.

Sterilize different things you contact normally, including:

- Computer keyboard and mouse
- House and vehicle keys
- Re-usable water bottles

- Steering of car
- Clothing pockets
- Door handles

Is it conceivable to be tainted by surfaces?

Note that there will be a contrast between a modest quantity of a virus that has been moved to a thing you contact and investing noteworthy energy within the sight of somebody who is effectively shedding the virus. With the last mentioned, the ailment weight will be more prominent and will make it harder for our safe framework to shield against. In any case, that doesn't mean we should disregard the previous either.

"Enjoy the pleasures just long enough to stay healthy."

(Baruch Spinoza)

"A smile is a curve that straightens everything."

(Phyllis Diller)

Chapter : 10
Vitamins for Strengthening Immunity

In recent decades, human energy consumption has decreased by 2–2.5 times, and food consumption should also have decreased, otherwise all this will result in overweight and illness. For example, in order to get the necessary daily intake of vitamin B 1.4 mg, you need to eat 700-800 g of bread from whole meal flour or a kilogram of lean meat. However, if the need for fats and carbohydrates decreased, then the need for vitamins and minerals remained the same, because they are necessary for the work of internal organs, the production of internal juices, good nerve conduction, etc. Even the most proper healthy diet, calculated for 2500 kilocalories per day, has deficiency in most vitamins, at least 20-30%.

When boiling milk, the amount of vitamins contained in it is significantly reduced.

On average, 9 months a year, Europeans eat vegetables grown in greenhouses or after long-term storage. Such foods have significantly lower levels of vitamins than open-field vegetables.

After 3 days of storage in the refrigerator, about 30% of vitamin C is lost. At room temperature, this figure is about 50%.

During the heat treatment of products, 25% to 90-100% of vitamins are lost.

In the light, vitamins are destroyed (vitamin B2 is very active), vitamin A is afraid of ultraviolet radiation.

Peeled vegetables contain significantly less vitamins.

Drying, freezing, machining, storage in metal utensils, pasteurization also very significantly reduce the content of vitamins in the starting products, even those that are traditionally considered sources of vitamins.

It is better to use vitamins not in the form of tablets, but as part of food products.

Vitamin E is very useful, it is especially important in preventing damage to cell membranes. It has a strong anti- inflammatory and immune-stimulating effect. It also helps to increase the production of interferon and reduce the incidence of acute respiratory infections. When interacting with selenium, the effectiveness of vitamin E is increased. It is abundant in nuts, seeds, whole grains and sweet potatoes (sweet potato).

Vitamin A deficiency weakens the body's immune response to foreign protein penetration. Sources of vitamin A: red and yellow vegetables and fruits (carrots, melons, tomatoes), as well as liver and eggs.

B vitamins help stimulate immune activity during periods of stress and breakdown. With a sharp drop in the level of B vitamins, the body's ability to produce antibodies to kill the infection also decreases significantly. Most of all B vitamins in yeast mushrooms, milk, cheese, liver.

Vitamin C increases the body's resistance to infection, as it contributes to the formation of specific antiviral antibodies, stimulates the production of its own interferon by the human body. That is why citrus fruits, currants, rosehips, sea buckthorn are so useful. A lack of vitamin C weakens the response of the body's defense systems to a signal about pathology, reduces the rate of antibody production to fight infection. It is found in large quantities in fresh fruits (especially kiwi, blackcurrant, rosehip, apples and citrus fruits), as well as in green vegetables (broccoli, spinach, leafy salads, cabbage, dill, parsley).

Vitamin D has not only an anthracitic effect; in recent years, its immune-stimulating effect has been proven. He is involved in the synthesis of interferon, increases the activity of natural killer cells. Most of all it contains fatty varieties of fish (or fish oil) and milk (and dairy products).

Vitamin PP stimulates phagocytosis (the destruction of pathogenic bacteria in the body). It is found in cereals: buckwheat, barley, rice and nuts: pistachios, peanuts, as well as in sunflower seeds.

Vitamin deficiency and their symptoms

Hypovitaminosis or vitamin deficiency is a disease that occurs due to a decrease in the amount of one or another vitamin in the body. Vitamin deficiency is the complete absence of any vitamin in the body. Vitamin deficiency is quite rare these days, but hypovitaminosis is quite common, which is facilitated by the diet of modern man.

To understand why the well-being worsens, work becomes harder and the mood decreases from any trifle you need to know the causes of hypovitamins and the symptoms that arise from them.

Reasons for development of vitamin deficiency

- hypovitaminosis A: predominant use of vegetable oils; a sharp deficit in the diet of animal foods rich in vitamin A, and plant foods rich in carotene; low protein content in food; hard physical work; great nervous tension; infectious diseases; chronic enterocolitis, diabetes mellitus, liver and thyroid disease;

- hypovitaminosis B: a uniform diet of fine-grained grain processing products; excess carbohydrates and proteins in food; chronic alcoholism and beer abuse; significant and prolonged consumption of raw fish (carp and herring); heavy physical work and nervous tension; staying in high temperature or cold; chronic bowel disease, diabetes mellitus, thyrotoxicosis;

- hypovitaminosis B: protein-poor nutrition; a sharp decrease in the consumption of milk and dairy products; physical and nervous stress; long-term use of drugs; diseases of the intestines, liver and pancreas;

- Hypovitaminosis B: long-term use of anti-TB drugs; chronic diseases of the gastrointestinal tract;

- Hypovitaminosis B (folic acid): destruction during heat treatment of products; chronic alcoholism; bowel disease (chronic enterocolitis); irrational treatment with antibiotics, sulfa drugs;

- Hypovitaminosis B: complete exclusion of animal products from food (passion for vegetarianism); the presence of worms; chronic alcoholism; diseases of the stomach and intestines (atrophic gastritis, chronic enterocolitis);

- hypovitaminosis C: when there are few fresh vegetables, fruits and berries in the diet; when, during improper storage or improper cooking, the vitamin is washed out of fruits and vegetables; mainly flour nutrition, insufficient protein content in food, great physical and nervous load;

- Hypovitaminosis D: insufficient formation of vitamin D in the skin with prolonged absence of the sun; long-term use of foods with a predominance of carbohydrates;

- Hypovitaminosis K: the exclusion of fats from food; diseases of the liver, biliary system, intestines; irrational treatment with antibiotics, sulfa drugs, anticoagulants;

- hypovitaminosis PP (nicotinic acid): unilateral nutrition using corn as the main product; low protein content in food;

solar radiation; long-term treatment with anti-TB drugs; chronic enterocolitis.

Signs of vitamin deficiency

- Hypovitaminosis A: dry skin, its thickening, keratinization (hyperkeratosis), a tendency to skin diseases. In infants diaper rash, thrush, stomatitis are observed. With a lack of vitamin A, tracheitis, bronchitis, gastroenteritis, colitis, and cystitis occur for a long time and are poorly treated. A person has night blindness, night blindness, conjunctivitis, in severe cases - up to complete blindness;

- Hypovitaminosis In a decrease in appetite, nausea, constipation, headaches, irritability, memory loss, peripheral polyneuritis, tachycardia, shortness of breath, pain in the heart, muscle weakness later join;

- hypovitaminosis B: damage to the mucous membrane of the lips with desquamation of the epithelium and cracks on the lips, stomatitis, inflammation of the tongue, skin lesions similar to eczema, conjunctivitis, photophobia, lacrimation, decreased vision, in children, growth and growth retardation;

- hypovitaminosis B: in children, growth retardation and weight gain, in adults and children, depression, apathy, weakness, burning sensation in the feet, intestinal dysfunction, respiratory tract infection, lowering blood pressure;

Hypovitaminosis B: irritability, drowsiness, impaired mental activity, peripheral neuritis, seborrheic dermatitis, stomatitis, conjunctivitis;

- hypovitaminosis B (folic acid): in children, delayed physical and mental development, growth, in adults and children macrocytic hyperchromic anemia, thrombocytopenia, impaired bowel function, dermatitis, impaired liver function, dry bright red tongue;

-    Hypovitaminosis B: diarrhea, decreased appetite, megalocytic hyperchromic anemia, tingling, burning of the tongue, redness of its tip, decreased acidity of gastric juice, impaired gait and sensitivity of the skin and muscles of the limbs, polyneuritis;

- Hypovitaminosis C: weakness, irritability, dryness and peeling of the skin, swelling of the gums, their bleeding, nosebleeds, pinpoint hemorrhages on the bends of the neck, limbs, pain in the lower extremities;

- Hypovitaminosis D: in children rickets (violation of the child's daytime and nighttime sleep, excessive sweating, undue anxiety, and decreased muscle tone. Later, deformations of the bones of the skull and chest (flattening of the neck, thickening of the costal cartilages at the junction with the bone parts of the ribs); in adults, osteoporosis (thinning of bone tissue);

- Hypovitaminosis E: muscle weakness, early muscle dystrophy;

- hypovitaminosis PP (nicotinic acid): pellagra, red spots with swelling and inflammation on the skin of the hands, rough, dark brown skin that peels off, enlarged swollen tongue of raspberry color; diarrhea; lesions of the nervous system.

Often there is often a deficiency of several vitamins. But the leading one is the deficiency of one vitamin with the corresponding symptoms. In much country, hypovitaminosis C and B often occurs; moreover, hypovitaminosis C is usually found in winter and spring.

However, it should be remembered that prolonged use, and even more than exceeding the dose of vitamin preparations, can do more harm than good.

Chapter 2. The interaction of vitamins and minerals

- Vitamin A allows the body to use the supply of iron found in the liver.

- Vitamin B increases the bioavailability of magnesium,

- Magnesium increases the amount of vitamin B, which has the ability to penetrate into cells.

- Boron stabilizes the body's intake of calcium, magnesium and phosphorus.

- Vitamin D is needed to absorb calcium.

- Vitamin D improves the absorption of phosphorus.

- Vitamin C improves the absorption of chromium.

- Copper improves absorption and increases the benefits brought by iron.

- Selenium enhances the antioxidant effect of vitamin E.

- Vitamin K contributes to calcium in bone building and proper blood coagulation.

Consequences of misuse of vitamins

A common mistake is the uncontrolled use of huge doses of ascorbic acid for the treatment of hypo- and vitamin deficiency C. With prolonged use of large doses of vitamin C (as part of vitamin complexes), the central nervous system (anxiety, feeling of heat, insomnia), inhibition of pancreatic function, and the appearance of sugar in the urine, due to excessive formation of oxalic acid, an adverse effect on the kidneys is possible, an increase in blood coagulability (blood clots) is possible. Hyper doses of vitamin C lead to increased loss of vitamins B from the body.

Moreover, the body quickly adapts and assimilates the rapid excretion of vitamin C.

Large doses of vitamin C are prohibited in patients with cataracts, in patients with diabetes, thrombophlebitis, and during pregnancy. A person needs a daily dose of vitamin C from 30 to 60 mg, pregnant and lactating - 90 mg.

A systematic prolonged excess of daily dosages of vitamins is dangerous because:

- with the introduction of massive doses of vitamins, protective mechanisms are turned on aimed at their elimination. The more a person drinks them, the less they are absorbed;

- fat-soluble vitamins have the ability to accumulate in the body and may have a toxic effect;

- the irrational use of large doses of vitamins can change the balance of vitamins, predisposing to the strengthening or provocation of hypovitaminosis;

- the introduction of a large amount of vitamin A increases the body's need for vitamins C and B and at the same time it is noted that vitamin C increases the conservation and concentration of vitamin B and reduces the level of vitamin A in the blood;

- the introduction of large doses of vitamin B increases the excretion of vitamin B;

- large doses of vitamin A increase the symptoms of hypovitaminosis D;

- an increase in the dose of vitamin C increases the excretion of both vitamin C and vitamin B.

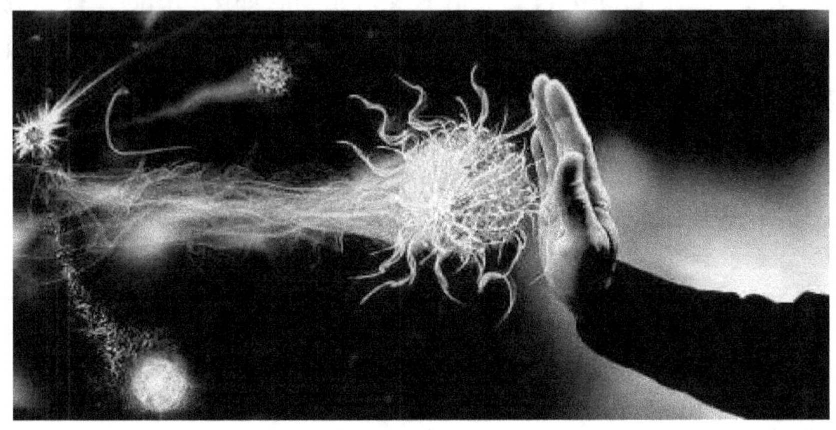

"When you're young and healthy, on Mondays you can think about killing yourself, and on Wednesdays you're laughing again."

(Marilyn Monroe)

"If everyone did it even once a day, give a smile, imagine what an incredible contagion of good humor would spread on earth."

(Marc Levy)

Chapter : 11
The Immune System

In this chapter we will discuss what the immune system is, what the main function of it is, the components and parts of your immune system, and how they operate together. After this, you will gain an understanding of what immunity is and how it is obtained. At the end of this chapter you will learn about some of the most common immune system disorders and diseases.

How does the immune system work and function

The immune system is a network of cells and tissues that run throughout the body. These cells have the ability to identify foreign tissue. Its main function is to remove faulty or dead cells that are present in the body, and more importantly, to keep harmful pathogens from attacking healthy cells. Pathogens can be extremely harmful and include bacterium, viruses, and parasites.

Our immune system operates through our blood cells. White blood cells work inside the body by looking out for danger or damage. They detect foreign cells by scanning the surface of cells and identifying proteins on the surface. When an unknown cell is recognized, a signal is sent to alert the rest of the system to prepare for an attack.

Main components of the immune system

The main components of the immune system consist of white blood cells, also referred to as leukocytes (Newman, 2018). They are found in the blood vessels, such as the lymphatic vessels, and circulate the body searching for pathogens. When a pathogen is found, a signal is sent to other cells.

White blood cells are stored in lymphoid organs, such as:

- Thymus
- Spleen
- Bone Marrow
- Lymph Nodes

There are two types of white blood cells: phagocytes and lymphocytes.

1. Phagocytes: White blood cells break down and absorb pathogens. There are several types, neutrophils, monocytes, macrophages, and mast cells (Newman, 2018).
2. Lymphocytes: These cells keep track of previous pathogen invasions so that they can easily recognize them if they were to appear again. Lymphocytes start out in the bone marrow. Many remain there and form B-lymphocytes or B-cells, which create antibodies. The remaining lymphocytes make their way to the thymus gland and transform into T-lymphocytes or T-cells. T- cells eliminate dangerous cells and alert leukocytes, otherwise called white cells, of invading pathogens (Newman, 2018). Two types of T-cells exist:

- Helper T-cells are responsible for the immune system's response, sending signals to other cells, stimulating B-cells, and attracting cell eating phagocytes (Newman, 2018).

- Cytotoxic T-lymphocytes, or killer T-cells, attack infected cells. They are important for fighting off viruses and recognizing all parts of a virus on cells (Newman, 2018).

Parts of the immune system

Every part of our immune system has a specific job to help fight off infections and to keep you healthy. They are located throughout the body and each part has sub-parts that are vital for proper functioning of the immune system.

Lymph Nodes

These are small bean shaped structures whose job is to create and catalog cells to protect against infections or diseases. They contain lymph, which is a clear fluid that carries cells' various parts in the body. The lymph nodes will expand and will feel sore when an infection is being fought.

Spleen

The largest lymphatic organ is the spleen. It is located under the ribs and just above the stomach and contains leukocytes that defend against infections and diseases. The spleen's job is to monitor levels of blood flowing through the body and clear poorly working cells (Zimmermann, 2018).

Bone Marrow

This is a tissue found within the bones and is where white cells are transmitted from. The bone marrow located in our hip bones and our thigh bones are of a spongy texture which store immature cells.

Thymus

This small organ is where T-cells mature and is not a well- known part of the immune system. This organ is located beneath the breast bone, and is of similar shape to a thyme leaf, which is how it received its name, thymus (Zimmermann, 2018). The primary role of this organ is to trigger or maintain the production of antibodies that can build up in muscle weakness. It is often larger in infants and continue to grow until puberty; only after puberty will it shrink, eventually being replaced with fat (Zimmermann, 2018).

How the immune system response functions

The immune system response is a process that occurs when white blood cells detect foreign proteins on a cell's surface. First, B-cells recognize foreign proteins, or antigens, as invaders (Newman, 2018). Most often, these are bacteria such as a virus, toxin, or fungus, but can also be detected as a faulty or dead cell. The B-cells will secrete antibodies once an antigen is found. Antibodies do not kill antigens, they just mark them so other cells, such as phagocytes, can destroy them.

How immunity works

Immunity is the buildup of stored antibodies in the body, so that when repeat antigens invade, they can be remembered and effectively attacked.

Types of Immunity

Innate: This is the type of immunity we are born with. The first barrier an invader has to surpass is the skin or mucous membranes, also known as external barriers into our body. Other barriers considered innate are: macrophages, neutrophils, dendritic cells, mast cells, stomach acid, enzymes, eosinophils, basophils, and chemicals like interferon and interleukin-1 (Zimmermann, 2018). They do not protect against specific threats.

Passive immunity: This immunity is not long lasting. This type of immunity is most common with babies, who obtain their antibodies from their mother before birth and from breast milk after birth. These antibodies are passed down from a mother to her child and provide the child with immunity against infections throughout the first few years of life (Newman, 2018). Simply put, this is a type of immunity that is borrowed and is not produced from one's own body.

Adaptive or acquired immunity: This type of immunity comes from antibodies that are stored in the body over the course of one's life. They protect against all pathogens one's system may encounter. The immune system easily identifies pathogens because copies of the antibodies have been kept in immunological memory, which is a library of antibodies (Newman, 2018).

Common immune system disorders

Diseases of the internal immune system are broadly defined and can consist of allergic diseases such as rhinitis, asthma, or eczema, which represent a hyper-response to external allergens. They can include the dysregulation of the system resulting in autoimmune diseases like lupus and RA, as well as disorders of the system that result in inflammatory diseases and cancer. A deficiency in the system, such as antibody deficiencies or cell mediated conditions, can also occur. Common immune system disorders include:

Immunodeficiency: Parts of the internal immune system stop responding. This can be caused by age, obesity, alcoholism, and malnutrition. Immunodeficiency can also be inherited. The most common immunodeficiency diseases include chronic granulomatous disease (CGB) and AIDS (Newman, 2018).

Autoimmunity: The system begins to attack healthy cells instead of cells that are invading the system. The most common autoimmune diseases are: celiac disease, Graves' disease, rheumatoid arthritis (RA), and type 1 diabetes, but many more also exist (Newman, 2018).

Hypersensitivity: The system reacts to tissue that is healthy, but slightly damaged. This is most common in the case of allergies (Newman, 2018). At times, the body can respond dangerously to the allergen, resulting in anaphylactic shock.

Diagnosis and treatments for immune system disease

Some symptoms of immune disorders can include fever and fatigue. Most disorders can be diagnosed through blood tests, which will measure the levels of immune elements and their functional activity (Zimmermann, 2018). Allergies are detected through blood or skin tests to identify which allergens trigger symptoms.

Treatment can include medications to help reduce the trigger of an immune response with overactive disorders. Another treatment option is replacing the missing immune elements. This can be done through antibody infusion, which assists our immune system to fight off infections (Zimmermann, 2018).

What are Infectious Diseases?

Infections occur when pathogens, such as bacteria or viruses, make their way into the body and cause harm. They use the body to sustain themselves, reproduce, and colonize. These pathogens can multiply and adapt quickly. When pathogen colonies become too overpowering for an immune system to defend against, the infections caused by pathogens become destructive because of the release of toxins that trigger negative responses throughout the body (Nordqvist, 2017).

Infections can spread and affect the body in different ways due to the differing agents. Infectious diseases can be transmitted by:

- Airborne particles
- Bodily fluids
- Fecal matter
- Skin contact
- Touching objects or a person who is infected

There are three groups of infections that can occur. They are listed below.

Viral infections

These are caused by a virus. Millions of viruses exist but only 5,000 have been identified (Nordqvist, 2017). They invade a host cell by attaching themselves to it and release their genetic material. This causes the cell to replicate, resulting in the virus multiplying. When the cell dies, a new virus is released and infects a new cell.

Not all viruses will destroy the host cell. Some change its functions. These changes can lead to cancer forcing the cells to replicate in an uncontrollable way (Nordqvist, 2017).

Common viral infections:

- Common cold caused by rhinovirus, coronavirus, or adenovirus.
- Encephalitis and meningitis are caused by the enterovirus or herpes virus.
- Warts, and other skin infections, are often the result of the human papillomavirus (HPV) or herpes simplex virus (HSV).
- Gastroenteritis is often caused by a norovirus.
- Human immunodeficiency virus (HIV)
- Polio
- Influenza
- Ebola

Antiviral medications are often prescribed but cannot halt a virus from multiplying. They also do not boost immunity. Antibiotics often increase the risk of antibiotic resistance. Treatments tend to relieve symptoms for an immune system so that it can combat a virus.

Bacterial infections

These are single celled microorganisms called prokaryotes. Nearly one nonillion bacterium can be found on Earth, which make up the Earth's biomass. Some live inside the body, in our gut and airways, and are harmless (Nordqvist, 2017). These are good bacteria. The body can become ill from either a bacterial disease or a bacterial infection.

The most common deadly bacterial diseases include:

- Bubonic plague
- Cholera
- Diphtheria
- Dysentery
- Pneumonia
- Tuberculosis
- Typhoid
- Typhus

The most common bacterial infections include:

- Bacterial meningitis
- Food poisoning
- Gastritis
- Pneumonia
- Sinusitis
- Skin infections
- Sexually transmitted diseases
- Tuberculosis
- Upper respiratory tract infections
- Urinary tract infections

Both bacterial diseases and infections require antibiotics, although some can be resilient to treatment and survive.

Fungal infections

Fungal infections are multicellular parasites, which absorb and decompose organic matter through enzymes. They are also capable of reproducing and spreading single-celled spores. Their structure, or hyphae, is usually cylindrical and long. They consist of small filament branches which protrude from the main structure. There are over 51 million fungi species in the world. Many fungal infections occur on the surface of our skin. Other times, it can progress under the surface of our skin. Inhaling fungal spores results in systemic infections that can disrupt the entire body (Nordqvist, 2017).

The most common fungal infections include:

- Valley fever, coccidioidomycosis
- Athlete's foot
- Ringworm
- Eye infections

Prevention of infectious diseases

Below is a list of ways to reduce the risk of infection:

- Wash your hands before and after preparing food, and when you are finished in the restroom.
- Clean surfaces that in contact with food.
- Stay up to date with vaccinations.
- Only take antibiotics when prescribed and continue to take them for the length prescribed. Do not stop taking antibiotics early because you are feeling better.
- Regularly disinfect rooms that are at higher risk of bacteria concentration, like the bathroom and the kitchen.
- Be smart about sex and get checked regularly for STDs.
- Do not share personal belongings like hair brushes, combs, toothbrushes, razors, utensils, and cups.

- Follow a doctor's instructions if traveling for work, so that you do not infect others.
- Maintain a healthy and active lifestyle to maintain a strong immune system.

Now that you have a basic understanding of how an immune system functions, and what can have a negative effect on it.

"Without my family, your help and support, I wouldn't have made it to be who I am."

(Michael Schumacher)

"One smile always gives birth to another smile. Heal only those who want to heal."

(Hippocrates)

Chapter :12
How to Protect Yourself and Others from Coronavirus

In this chapter we will list the best methods you can use to protect yourself and people you care about from the Coronavirus.

First of all, the coronavirus was transmitted from animals to humans. So if you have to eat meat, eggs or other food derived from animals, do yourself the favor of cooking them more than thoroughly.

Heat and high temperatures are the best and easiest way to get rid of microbes and bacteria.

For this same exact reason, a good tip is to avoid animal markets as much as possible.

The virus started there and their hygienic conditions are poor especially when animals are slaughtered there.

So, what can we do about the Coronavirus?

As we already know, there is no vaccine available yet or a definitive cure, but there are some steps we can take in order to prevent it:

- Treat it like it's a common cold;

Avoiding cold or freezing conditions is a great move to avoid the Coronavirus itself.

- Wash your hands with soap;

Take care of your personal hygiene and wash your hands often with soap and water, it is ideal to avoid the infection of germs, especially after being on public transport.

- Drink a lot of fluids and water;

Staying hydrated is an excellent remedy to keep your body and immune system active and at full power, it will help you decrease your chances of getting sick.

- Use a humidifier or hot showers;

A humidifier or a hot shower is an excellent remedy to help treat sore throats and coughs.

- Take time to rest;

Keeping the body well rested is a great way to preserve your health and immune system.

- Avoid contact with sick people, especially with infected patients;

Avoid contact as much as possible. It goes without saying, but we must avoid any kind of contact with people who may be infected or show any kind of symptom associated to the Coronavirus.

- Cover your mouth and nose when you cough and disinfect any object you may you have touched;

To avoid spreading germs, it is very useful to cover your nose and mouth with a cloth or napkin when coughing.

- Contact your doctor;

If you are worried about your health and are suspicious of certain symptoms you are showing, it is highly recommended to contact your doctor for help and further instructions after receiving a proper diagnosis.

If your doctor also suspects that you may have the Coronavirus, as well as visiting a specialized hospital (your doctor will refer you to them) you should wear and walk around with a surgical mask as advised by the CDC.

Let's clarify something about the masks. You may be a bit skeptical about them, "Do they really work?"

As stated by countless specialists and doctors, masks, even if they're cheap, can actually help prevent infectious diseases and avoid their contagion (obviously, provided that they are used correctly and consistently).

Masks can block most airborne infectious particles as well as avoid you getting in direct contact with other people's coughs and sneezes.

A study conducted on SARS, also, shows that the constant use of masks or other respiratory protection used by workers and healthcare workers can reduce the risk of infection by up to 85%, which is a lot.

One very important detail, for which China could not prepare itself properly before the outbreak but we can, is that the risk of infection can be much lower if we all start wearing and using masks or other airways protections from now on, correctly and constantly when in public.

- What can you do to protect others?

It's fairly obvious that you should focus on all of the solutions above and apply them to yourself and members of your family or others of note close to you.

By protecting ourselves, we are already protecting others.

If a person close to us or living with us has symptoms similar to a common cold or the coronavirus, then it will be positive both for them and for us to make sure that they're applying all of the methods listed above to reduce the risk of infection and worsening of the illness as much as possible.

If we are the ones who have cold-like symptoms, here are some tricks to use to protect people around us effectively:

- Don't go out more than needed or leave the country;

-Stay at home while you're sick and try to isolate yourself;

- Avoid any kind of contact, especially close physical contact;

- Remember to cover your mouth and nose with a tissue or a piece of cloth when you sneeze or cough. Then throw away that tissue in the trash, get rid of the trash and wash your hands;

- Don't touch object and surfaces. If you touch them, then clean and disinfect them;

These are the best known remedies currently.

Follow them, avoid the illness and protect yourself and others.

Protect yourself and your family

World Health Organization has recommended standard practices for the general public to drastically reduce exposure and transmission to different range of diseases. They are summarized as Hand and respiratory hygiene as well as safe food practices.

- Please ensure you cover mouth and nose with flexed elbow or tissue when sneezing or coughing – dispose the tissue immediately and wash your hands thoroughly.
- Clean hands regularly by using alcohol-based hand rub or soap and water;
- Please avoid direct contact with anyone suffering from fever and cough;

- When visiting markets situated in areas where there is outbreak of novel coronavirus. Please avoid unprotected direct contact with live animals and also surface contact with animals.

- If you are suffering from cough, fever and have difficulty in breathing. You are advised to seek for medical assistance as soon as possible. Also ensure you share your past travel history with your doctor.

- You should avoid eating raw or half cooked animal products. Raw meat, animal organs or milk should be handled with great care to avert cross contamination with uncooked foods and ensure you observe good food safety practices.

You, your dog and the coronavirus

When a virus like this seems to spread so quickly, it can be more than a little scary. Hence, as dog lovers, we often turn to our pups during these times. If you have been familiar with the phrase, then, you must have questions such as "Can my dog get coronavirus?" or "can I give my dog coronavirus?" first, don't panic. But bear in mind that the novel coronavirus (also known as Wuhan coronavirus or nCoV) is being linked to snakes sold at the market. Thus, we can conclude that animals carrying the virus can pass it to a human host via meat consumption. *the center for disease control continues to research this fact. Also, while there is a canine coronavirus disease, it isn't linked to this strain. The canine coronavirus's name has similar characteristics to how human viruses get theirs. It's round, crown-like appearance when you look at it with an electron microscope. Dogs get stricken by this virus when they eat poop that contains the virus.

The more reason you should keep your dog's mouth away from any pile around.

Symptoms of this coronavirus in dogs

Often, there are hardly any symptoms in dogs. In rare cases, when there are symptoms, you may observe poor appetite and the onset of diarrhea along with lethargy. There might be blood or mucus in your dog's diarrhea. The symptoms may become more severe if your dog is suffering from another disease (such as parvovirus) before contracting this infection. However, these symptoms may be caused by other issues. Hence, your best option is to take your dog to his veterinary doctor. As of this writing, there have been no reported cases of the 2019-CoV in dogs. But human-animal contact was identified as the cause of the previous strains of coronavirus. Human contact with MERS from dromedary camels and civet cats appears to be the cause of the SARS-CoV. The virus causes respiratory issues after it infects the human host. It often spreads from human-to-human through the air during a sneeze or cough.

Can you give your dog coronavirus?

The SARS coronavirus is proof that mammals such as civet cats and camels can be stricken with coronavirus to infect humans. However, there is no proof that 'coronavirused' humans can infect their pets with this virus. Your first defense remains good hygiene practices - cover your mouth when you sneeze and wash your hands regularly. Protect your dog by preventing him from eating poop. Then, when he's through with his business, pick up after him and bathe him regularly.

"The war must be prepared in time to win faster!"

(Publilio Siro)

"It takes seventy-two muscles to pout but only twelve to Smile. Try it for once."
(Mordecai Richler)

Chapter :13
How to Prepare
Quarantines

If there was a quarantine in your country like we see in China, where they quarantine millions of people in multiple cities, are you prepared for that? Ask yourself that question.

If next week the government will ask people to stay indoors are you ready for that?

Ask yourself that question and what kind of supplies you would need if you were to be in a quarantined environment, if you had to stay home or stay indoors. Do you have enough supplies on hand, so you don't have to run out and go to the store or go to a National Guard food facility where they're going to be handing out food?

Now is the time to take inventory of all your supplies and determine if you have everything that you need. Don't wait until there's a quarantine ordered, then it's too late because everybody's going to be running to the stores and panic buying food and panic buying water and within a day or two everything is going to be cleaned out.

So, you need to start thinking about it now, while there's still some time left because all indications are pointing towards the possibility of a pandemic. This virus could very well explode in western countries like exploded in China, because it seems to be very contagious.

Now is the time to start getting ready and to think about all the different supplies you would need: food, water, shelter, self-defense, medical supplies, sanitation supplies, any kind of tools that you think you would need during a quarantine scenario. In this way you can bunker in your house for a couple of weeks and not have to go to the outside world to get supplies once there are people sick everywhere and the risk of getting sick is going up.

Make sure you have plenty of food on hand at least a month or two of food. I would say ideally six months or more but if you're just starting out you should order at least a month of food because if they order a quarantine, they make quarantine and ask people to stay indoors at least a couple of weeks. You should have at least 20 or 30 gallons (90 to 130 Liters) of water on hand at all times in your home. At that time, you don't really want to have to run out to the store because then you can possibly expose yourself to the virus.

It's not about fear mongering you, I'm just saying that we should always be prepared for the worst. This way, if nothing happens you have your freeze-dried food and you don't need it. You could eat that food even if nothing happened.

Stock food

FEMA recommends at a minimum a three-day food supply to support you and your family during an emergency.

The great thing about items we are discussing is that they are items that you use anyway and by purchasing extra they'll get used eventually so you're not getting items that are going to be wasted.

Items I suggest for your two-week pantry.

Which are the criteria to select your pantry food items? Food must be easy to cook and easy to store for a decent amount of time without refrigeration. We should prefer items that are already part of our daily meals, food items that require a little electricity or fuel to prepare and they need to provide ample nutrition and contain little salt.

Let's consider this list as a bare minimum starting point and the items in this list obviously change in relation to the size of your family. I'm considering a typical family of four (two adults and two children).

1. **Rice.** You can choose brown or white rice. I prefer the brown one for his nutritional value and I would suggest around 20 pounds (10 kg).
2. **Beans.** There's a lot of options based on your taste. I'd suggest about 20 pounds (10kg) of dried beans.

Now rice is rich in starch and it's an excellent source of energy while beans are rich in protein and contain other minerals. These two items are stapled foods around the world and combined together they're a great source of amino acids.

3. **Canned meat.** You can start with 20 cans of chicken meat or tuna or the kind of meat you prefer. The number of cans depends on their size.
4. **Canned fruit.**
5. **Canned vegetables.** Green beans, corn and tomatoes and again I'd recommend probably around 20 cans, depending on their size.

6. **Soup.** It's great because it's something that you can cook up really quickly with little to no preparation.

7. **Powdered milk.** It can serve a lot of purposes, it's nutritious and it's just great comfort food.

8. **Cereal.** Combine this with powdered milk and you've got an easy breakfast.

9. **Oatmeal.** You can throw in some fruits, peanut, butter or powdered milk and you've got a solid breakfast.

10. **Peanut butter.** A couple of large jars of peanut butter is a really popular option. It has got high protein and it's something that will help you kind of keep hunger at bay.

11. **Pancake mix.** Storing about ten pounds of this you can toss Jam or syrup on this and you've got a great meal.

12. **Honey, jam or syrup** are all great sweeteners for various food items we mention on this list. I keep a couple of jars of jams and storage along with about ten pounds of honey and a couple of different syrup options. They are great kind of comfort food and a psychological boost.

13. **Pasta.** Keep around 20 pounds. There's a lot of different options.

14. **Spaghetti sauce**. Keep around about 10 jars.

15. **Salt.** This is a necessary mineral that your body needs to operate and it enhances the flavor of your food.

16. **Oil.** Olive oil and a few other options. Oil serves many purposes and cooking and the great thing about it is that it helps us satiate hunger.

17. **Coffee and/or tea.**

18. **Spices and condiments.** Things like Tabasco sauce, salsa pepper or other options that just help add variety to your diet and just prevent you know fatigue of having to eat certain foods over and over.

19. **Nuts**. This is easy comfort food you can quickly grab, source of protein, source of fat

20. **Packaged meal.** Something like macaroni and cheese, just some easy comfort foods for children, easy to cook and prepare. Also consider convenience foods that are easy to grab and eat and don't necessarily require a lot of preparation like protein bars or crackers and be sure to actually try these foods out before stocking them up.

Have a place to store food, put items with an expiration date that's further in the future at the back and items that need to be eaten sooner to the front. Be sure as well to have a pen and paper in the storage area to write down items you need to replace on your next trip to the store. Buy what you eat, rotate and repeat.

Finally, make sure you have enough water stored up. People often underestimate how much water they're going to need.

Prepare your house

When a pandemic hits governments and medical experts usually advise people to stay in their homes and avoid contact with other people. If the outbreak is severe governments may be inclined to make it a widespread order to try and contain the disease and prevent it from spreading. If you're gonna be required to stay in your house for a prolonged period of time you need to make sure that it is well prepared.

Make sure to have a dedicated room that has a door or at least a plastic shower curtain to ensure that it's separated from the rest of the house and be sure to clean the room daily using bleach.

Your house will also need to have an area where you can store at least three weeks' supply of food and water (if you want to store more supply you are welcome!).

Stock items

1. **Home Equipment:** first-aid kit, battery-operated radio, simple backup power system like a small gas or solar generator, flashlights, medical book and other medical information you might need, household items and cleaning supplies (Kleenex, hand sanitizer and soap,

garbage bags, disposable plastic gloves, bleach or any surface cleaner) and toilet paper.

2. **Protective Items for Outdoor**: coverall suit, glasses, gloves, mask. Make a big supply of these items because you must waste the equipment each time you use it before coming into your house.

3. **Medicine** is one of the most important supplies that you need to have on hand. **Consult a doctor before taking any drug.**

4. **Supplies for your pets** if you have any (food, medicines and other items).

5. **Books, toys or other entertainment items** because you could have to stay home for many days or even weeks.

Create an emergency plan

It is important that you also have an emergency plan prepared in case things get worse. One important emergency plan that you need to have is caring for your kids if you have any. When a pandemic strikes schools and daycares will be closed for a prolonged period. This could be a problem if you are still required to come back to work during this scenario. You should have an **emergency fund** that can sustain you and your family for a certain period of time in case you need to stop working during the pandemic. Gather information on how your company handles pandemic situations so you'll know what you can and cannot do during the emergency. You can talk to close family member's friend's neighbors or even the community to help you care for your children in case the pandemic happens. Try to find information on how the local government or community can provide assistance during the pandemic so you can factor that into your decision.

Another emergency plan that you need to consider is an **evacuation plan** in case you need to leave your home to go somewhere safer. You cannot rule out the possibility that you and your family may need to go somewhere that is safer and you should know when it is the right time to evacuate or leave your city or town. It could be when the neighboring town or city is already experiencing the pandemic or when someone in your town is affected by the disease. This is a decision you'll need to make in advance. Identify places that you and your family can go that are not already impacted by the pandemic, if you have relatives or friends in the city or town that can help you, or you have a remote location or cabin that you can get to before your area's quarantine. Decide on what form of transportation you will use and have alternative routes in the event the main roads are closed off. You should also plan what you need to bring and how long you should stay in your secondary location.

Be sure to **have a plan in place in case you or someone in your family becomes infected**. Will you take them to the hospital or treat them at home? What assistance can your local government or medical experts provide? Surely hospitalization is required, but you should plan in advance in which hospital you would like you or your family members will be treated.

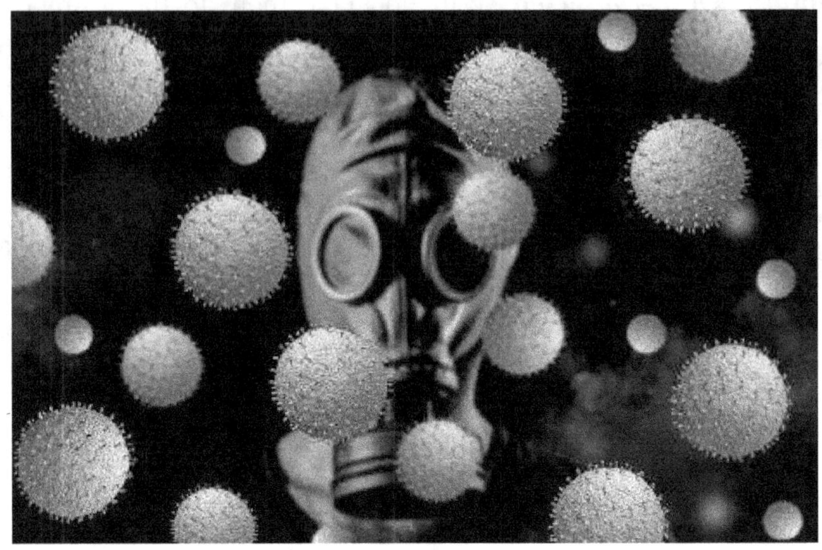

"Health has never produced anything. Misery is a gift. I only eat to feed the pain. Preparation for death takes a lifetime."

(Alda Merini)

"The sensual man often laughs where there's nothing to laugh about. Whatever stimulates him, his intimate well-being comes out."

(Johann Wolfgang Goethe)

Chapter : 14
Safety and Protection in a Pandemic

What you're going to need after you have a plan to provide food, shelter and other basic needs for yourself and your family is to make sure that you have what you need to keep from getting the virus.

You're going to also need a way to protect your personal safety. Whenever a pandemic occurs, there is often a collapse of certain societal norms - such as the ability to get food and water, gas and even money.

When that happens, there can be factions of people who decide that they're going walk outside of the boundaries of the law and take what they need. Some people are opportunists who will hunt for other people that they can prey on.

Safety items you need

Because the Coronavirus virus can spread so quickly and be so devastating when it touches a life, you need to be prepared for all of the ways that the virus can come at you.

The first item that you're going to need will be a supply of the N95 masks. You'll need these for every member of your family. You can find these in packages with a few or with plenty at medical supply stores, but since you're going to want to buy them in bulk, your best bet is to order them online.

Plus, you'll save money getting them online over the higher cost of buying them at a medical store. Figure that you need at least several months' worth of masks for every person who will need to wear one.

You'll want a supply that will last you 3 months at minimum but planning for longer (a year or two) is better. If a year seems excessive, all you have to do is take a look at the current outbreak.

It actually began in December with the host victim but wasn't properly recognized as the Coronavirus virus until March. It's raged on for an additional five months since then, bringing the total time the virus has run rampant among people to a total of nine months so far - but it's still not controlled.

This is why getting enough masks for a year minimum is the best way to make sure your family's safety is taken care of. When you wear the masks, you'll want to make sure that the areas around the mask seal well to your face.

You don't want any openings at all because the Coronavirus virus can get into your body through any mucus membrane area. So if you have to seal around the mask with tape to make sure it's secure, then do that.

You can also find these masks with filters in them - but they're more expensive. Whatever kind of mask you get, you want to make sure that you don't try to fit an adult sized mask onto a child.

There's too much room for error that way. There are separate masks made just for children that you can buy, so get them a minimum of a year's supply as well if you can.

You might have seen articles telling you that you should wear safety glasses in order to protect your eyes from being an entry point for the Coronavirus virus. But you should only use safety glasses as a last resort.

These are open on the sides and fluid from a contaminated individual can splash up and catch you in the corner of the eye where you're not protected. Instead of safety glasses, you'll want to purchase safety goggles.

These come with a rubber seal around the sides of them so they'll adhere to your face and offer you more protection that a simple pair of safety glasses will. But if you can't get the goggles, then anything is better than nothing.

Don't forget to make sure you get some kid sized ones to protect the children in your family. Outerwear is also paramount to your protection during a pandemic. There are two kinds of outerwear that you can get.

You can buy the disposable kind or the heavy duty plastic kind, re-usable kind. You might see these listed as chemical protection suits or training suits. If they have that label, it means that those are the suits that are used in dangerous situations like where there's been a chemical spill or the rough places where a first responder might need to go to help someone.

These suits can be very expensive, often costing a couple of hundred dollars or more. There are pros and cons to both kinds of suits. The disposable suits usually have sleeves and pant legs that have strong elastic in them so that they fit pretty snugly against your skin in order to keep out any viruses.

Some of these suits also come with fitted hoods so that you can cover the sides of your face to keep your ears protected. The strength and durability of the disposable hazmat suits depend on the brand that you buy and what the fabric consists of.

Some are more resistant to tears and breakdowns than other brands are. So always choose a brand that has a good track record for being resistant to tears. When you're done using these, you have to dispose of them properly so that any germs on the suit aren't carried back with you once you remove the outerwear.

The heavy duty hazmat suits have to be decontaminated after use and if you're not set up to deal with a contamination area without accidentally infecting yourself, then you'll want to go with the disposable suits.

Some of the heavy duty hazmat suits come with extras already attached - such as the gloves you'll need to use to protect yourself. You'll need to have plenty of gloves on hand and these can't be those flimsy household gloves like the thin cleaning gloves you find at the grocery store.

Those nick and tear open at the fingertips far too easily. They can't stand up to long use, either. You don't want to cover your body with a sturdy hazmat suit and then jeopardize yourself by choosing cheap gloves.

Protection is a must

You'll need to be aware of any late breaking news in the event of a pandemic. Since you may not be able to count on society working the way it has, you'll need to make sure that you have items that don't rely on an electricity infrastructure to operate.

Emergency broadcasts will still be done - even if society breaks down during a pandemic. So you'll want to make sure that you have a solar powered radio. You'll also want to make sure that you have solar powered flashlights and light sticks so that you can see in the event of blackouts.

You'll need a means of keeping in contact with others. Even if electricity is down, that doesn't mean you can't use your phone. There are solar powered units that can keep a cell phone charged up so that you can communicate with family members who may not be near you.

You also want to make sure that you have a way to communicate with any medical personnel if you have to. That's where the cell phone or a two-way radio can come in handy.

You'll need items that will help you start a fire and you'll need a backpack that contains first aid equipment and personal hygiene items. Besides what you need to survive, you'll also need protection of a different sort.

Having a multi-purpose knife on hand can help you accomplish a variety of tasks you might need to do. It can help you cut twine to string up a thermal blanket as a shelter if you need to in a pinch.

But a knife can also give you protection and even save your life if the need arises. Regardless of how you feel about weapons, you will need a way to take care of your personal safety.

When a pandemic hits, there will always be someone who will be caught without supplies. These people will take yours - and worse - if you don't have a way to defend yourself.

One of these means can be a knife. You can choose from knives like a tactical knife or a jungle knife. If you're not sure which kind of knife you want to have on hand, you can search for survival knives and choose one that's best for you.

You'll also need to have at least one gun. More is better - and you'll need the ammunition to go along with that weapon. Long rifles can be used for protection, but they can also be used to hunt for food so that you can have meat with your food supply in the event that you need it.

You'll also want to carry a personal handgun on a hip holster with you at all times in the event that lawlessness breaks out. You can get a small gun and some people like to go with a 9mm, a .38 or a .45.

You may never need to use any of the weapons to protect yourself or your loved ones, but you'll be glad that you have them if an event does occur in which you have to fight back.

"To be alive meant to breathe air; to breathe air meant to breathe open air."

(Paul Auster)

"What the sun is for flowers, smiles are for humanity."
(Joseph Addison)

Chapter : 15
Home Treatment for People with Acute Respiratory Illness

It will not be possible to deliver urgent or outpatient medical services to those who may need them during a public-health emergency, such as a pandemic. In fact, outpatient clinics will not be able to satisfy the need for hospital services and will not be able to deliver treatment to the most chronically ill patients.

Infection prevention so management for home environment COVID 2019 can quickly spread within a household. Someone who has not been diagnosed previously would be at risk of infection if they come into contact with a COVID patient.

Therefore, members of the household should follow the following recommendations:

- If a member of the household shows symptoms of COVID, including fever, cough, sore throat and trouble breathing, they should follow advice from public health. Restrict as much interaction as possible with the diseased person. Live in another room or live as far away from the sick party as possible (e.g., sleeping in a different bed) if this is not possible.
- Maintain properly ventilated public areas (e.g., showers, kitchen and bathroom) (e.g. leave windows open).
- When the sick person needs to be handled carefully, ensure that the injured person protects his or her mouth or nose with hands or other items (e.g. gloves, handkerchiefs or, if available, masks);
- Discard or disinfect items used to protect the mouth or nose properly.
- Should not interact inappropriately with body fluids. If touch happens, do grooming of the hand directly afterward.
- Hygiene of the hands, either by brushing with soap and water or by using hand rubbing based on alcohol. Tackle health issues (e.g., accidental consumption and

fire hazards) before prescribing household alcohol- based hand rubs.

- Ensure that someone at heightened risk of serious illness should not care for the sick or come in direct touch with the injured person.
- Prevent certain forms of potential access to the sick or infected items, such as exchanging of toothbrushes, cigarettes, utensils, foods, blankets, washcloths or bed linen.

Ensure that caregivers with serious COVID issues restrict their interaction with each other and follow national or state policy on home quarantine guidelines. Wherever practicable, the caregiver often uses a surgical mask or the best available nasal droplet cover when in direct contact with the sick person and performs hand washing procedures if a patient with an ARI is sick with a specific problem

- Notify the health care provider of the condition and provide guidance as to where to provide treatment, whether and when to visit.
- If necessary stop public transport; call an ambulance to hold a sick passenger in his own vehicle and open the vehicle's door.
- Do respiratory grooming at all times.

- Stand or sit as far apart as possible from others (at least 1 m), both in transit and in the health center.
- Using hand grooming whenever possible.

Facial protection: Using facial protection like a surgical mask and eye shielding (face cover or goggles) to secure the conjunctivae and mucous membranes of the nose, eyes and mouth during movements that are likely to cause blood splashes or sprays, bodily fluids, secretions or excretions. Use eye safety when delivering care in direct proximity with a patient with respiratory problems (e.g., coughing or sneezing), since there can be sprays of secretions.

Gowns • Wear gowns to shield the skin and avoid clothes from soiling during practices that are likely to cause blood splashes or sprays, bodily oils, secretions or excretions.

- Select a gown fitting for the operation and the quantity of fluid expected to be found. Unless the uniform in use is not moisture resistant, whether splashing or leakage of highly contagious material is expected to wear a protective apron over the uniform.
- Remove the soiled gown as quickly as possible, put it (as appropriate) in a waste or laundry receptacle and practice hand hygiene.

Management of health care facilities should encourage respiratory hygiene as follows:

- Enable all health care staff, patients and COVID family members to use respiratory hygiene.
- Educate health care staff, patients, family members and tourists about the value of removing nasal aerosols and secretions to help deter COVID-2019 infections from being spread.
- Recommend offering physical hygiene services (e.g. alcohol-based hand latex dispensers and hand- washing supplies) and respiratory hygiene (e.g., tissues); consider collecting places such as waiting rooms.

Coronavirus Disease 2019 versus the Flu

Influenza ("the flu"), and COVID-19, the disease caused by the current coronavirus, are also respiratory infectious diseases. Though the effects of COVID-19 and flu can appear identical, different viruses cause the two illnesses.

As of Feb. 26, 2020, flu showed far more of an effect on Americans than COVID-19. Current information on COVID-19 can be found at the Centers for Disease Control and Prevention (CDC). Let's discuss how the flu and COVID-19 are related and how they vary.

Similarities:

COVID-19 and the effects of flu each cause fever, cough, muscle aches, exhaustion, vomiting, and diarrhea at times. In exceptional cases, it can be moderate to severe, even fatal. May induce pneumonia.

Transmission

These can be transmitted from person to person by droplets in the air from coughing, sneezing, or talking to an affected person.

 A potential difference: COVID-19 could travel across the airborne route .An infectious person will carry flu for several days before their symptoms show, and COVID-19 is believed to be circulating in the same manner, though we don't know for sure yet.

Treatment: No virus can be treated with antibiotics that function only on bacterial infections.

Both should be treated by treating symptoms, such as fever reduction. Severe conditions, such as artificial ventilation, can require hospitalization and assistance.

Prevention This can be avoided by a regular, thorough washing of hands, coughing into the elbow's crook, remaining home while sick, and avoiding contact with infectious people.

Differences: COVID-19 and the Flu Cause COVID-19: The novel 2019 coronavirus, also known as serious acute respiratory syndrome coronavirus 2, or SARS-CoV-2 is caused by one virus.

Flu: Caused by some of the different influenza virus forms and strains.

Transmission Although both the flu and COVID-19 can be distributed in similar ways, there is still a potential difference: COVID-19 could travel via the airborne pathway, suggesting that tiny droplets left in the air could cause sickness in others well after the sick person is no longer nearby.

Antiviral drugs COVID-19: Antiviral drugs are currently conducting studies to see whether they can cure symptoms.

Flu: Antiviral medications can treat symptoms and sometimes shorten the disease's duration.

Vaccine COVID-19: There is currently no vaccine available, but research is underway.

Flu: A vaccine is available that is effective in avoiding any of the more harmful varieties or in reducing flu intensity.

COVID-19 infections: about 81,322 cases worldwide; 59 cases in the US as of Feb. 26, 2020.

Flu: Worldwide estimated to be 1 billion cases; US expected to be 9.3 million to 45 million cases a year.

Deaths COVID-19: about 2,770 deaths recorded worldwide; 0 deaths in the United States, as of Feb. 26, 2020.

Flu: 291,000 to 646,000 deaths worldwide; US deaths of 12,000 to 61,000 a year

"There are more important things in life than money. The trouble is, it takes money to buy them!"

(Groucho Marx)

"He who never laughs is not a serious person."
(Fryderyk Chopin)

Chapter : 16
What Supplies Will You Need?

This represented a big change in tone from earlier comments about COVID-19. As a result, this chapter has been added to help people learn more about how to prepare. The information presented here is primarily based on existing U.S. emergency preparedness guidelines, along with some tweaks based on how things have rolled out in China.

"We are asking the American public to prepare for the expectation that this might be bad...Now is the time for businesses, hospitals, communities, schools, and everyday people to begin preparing." – Dr. Nancy Messionnier, director of the CDC.

China hadn't experienced any notable issues with electrical disruptions or water issues from late-December 2019 to early-March 2020. With this in mind, the rest of the world can expect similar results. An exception to this may occur if the situation drags on for several months in a specific area. With that in mind, it's best to have plenty of food and water on hand.

- The CDC recommends at least 1 gallon of water per person, per day. But because we can't know how long a potential lockdown will go on or if the water will even be affected, it's hard to gauge how much to have on hand. You should always have two to three days of water on hand, but you may want to expand that to two to three weeks, if possible.

- Dry goods and canned food are best for emergencies because they don't require electricity for storage and won't go bad quickly. Some items to potentially stock up on include: canned vegetables, beans, pasta, cereal, powdered milk or stable-shelf milk/milk alternative, peanut butter, etc. Again, you should always keep a supply good for two to three days on hand for any emergency situation. In this particular case, government representatives from around the world have recommended everything from one to six weeks' worth of food as a good guideline.

- Don't forget about your pets! They will also need food and water for the same time period.

- If possible, get a 90-day supply of any current prescription medications. Don't forget to also grab extras of any over-the-counter meds that you use on a regular basis, along with medication that can help treat the cough and fever that often accompanies COVID-19.

- Face masks may eventually become necessary but hoarding them won't help others and may make it harder for the healthcare system to do its job. Additionally, finding face masks right now is very difficult. Keep in mind that people who are immunocompromised and/or taking certain prescription medications may need to wear a mask out in public, regardless of any illnesses or outbreaks.

- Hand sanitizer, bleach, Lysol spray, hand soap, and other cleaning products are a good thing to keep well stocked.

- You'll want to ensure you have plenty of toilet paper for everyone in the house.

- Don't forget about your mental and emotional needs. In the event of a lockdown, you'll need a way to pass the time. Consider books, crossword puzzles, board games, adult coloring books, movies, and anything else that will help keep your mind off the situation.

- Your physical needs are also very important. If your area is going to be locked down, try to grab some fresh fruit and vegetables to help you get through the first few days. You should also consider how you can use items inside your home to keep your body physically fit in the unlikely instance of an extended lockdown. In China, people have used water jugs and other household items as makeshift weights.

- Keep calm. Stress makes you more likely to catch a virus. Just remember that no matter what happens, the vast majority of people will be okay. In fact, studies have indicated so far that approximately 80 percent of coronavirus patients have a mild enough case that they need little to no medical care.

Food and water

This one seems pretty basic, right? We all need food and water to survive. But what kind of food we should buy may not be as intuitive, especially if you don't have a lot of extra money to buy more supplies than your normal budget would allow. One good thing about a disease pandemic, as opposed to other types of natural disasters, is that you are not likely to lose your access to water and electricity, so while prepping for those types of disasters is a good idea too, those are two key necessities you shouldn't have to worry too much about in this situation. But how much food will you need and what kind of food?

First, think about how many people you will need to feed and what your normal eating habits are like. Do you eat three meals a day regularly? Maybe you eat two meals per day and do a lot of snacking in between? Whatever your habits may be, it is commonly advised that you have an extra two weeks supply of food on hand. My suggestion, however, is that you have at least an extra one-month supply of food available and it doesn't hurt to have a two- to three-month supply if you have space and money to do so.

When it comes to what kind of food to store, there are many options. Many companies specialize in creating freeze-dried or dehydrated, just add water, meals that have a shelf life of up to 25 years. You can purchase these in individual packages, in bulk, or buckets that contain a variety of different meals. Some of the more popular companies that sell these products are Wise Foods Company, Mountain House, and Augason Farms. I have used products from each of these companies on camping trips because freeze-dried foods are light and compact making them perfect for backpacking. Hopefully, we won't see price gouging in times like these but to give a frame of reference, I see a 30 day/1-person supply emergency food bucket listed on Amazon right now for $170.00. That might seem expensive but that comes to less than $6.00 per day.

If you're like me and you have eaten a good bit of dehydrated meals like this on camping trips in the past, you know that you are going to get pretty tired of it. That is why I recommend also stocking up on other, more common foods that you may already be used to buying. The most important things to consider are buying foods that a.) have the nutrients, vitamins, and protein that you need to stay healthy, and b.) have a long shelf life and won't go bad before you can eat them.

Below is a list of some cheap foods with a long shelf life that you may want to consider:

- Dried Beans
- Rolled Oats
- Rice
- Dehydrated fruits
- Pastas
- Canned Beans
- Peanut Butter
- Crackers

- Potato Flakes
- Dried Meats like Jerky
- Coconut Oil
- Sugar
- Honey
- Salt and Pepper
- Coffee
- Cereals
- Canned Foods
- Energy bars like Cliff Bars
- Bouillon Products
- Alcohol
- Canned Tuna and Salmon
- Pancake Mix

Of course, there are many options that fall into this category and everyone likes to eat different things, so get a good mix of items to keep everyone well-fed and happy. Also, consider having at least a few good treats on hand if you have small children that may have a harder time adjusting to a new routine at home.

When it comes to water, again, it shouldn't be as much of an issue in dealing with a disease pandemic as it would in other situations like a natural disaster, but it is always a good idea to have extra clean water on hand or alternatively, reliable filtration system. One of the cheapest and easiest systems today is the Lifestraw or bottles that incorporate some version of a straw filter. Having a few of these on hand is a great backup for situations where clean water is unavailable. There are also many different sizes of filtration systems available from compact and lightweight systems meant for camping to larger systems that can filter much more water in a shorter period of time.

Medicines

You should have an extra supply of any medications that you might need. Non-prescription medications like pain relievers, fever reducers, cold and cough medicines, stomach remedies, vitamins and other supplements should be on hand. Also having drinks rich in electrolytes or even Pedialyte is a good idea in case anyone is experiencing dehydration due to illness. If you have small children, make sure you have specially formulated medications for them rather than giving them small doses of adult medications. Even if you are under quarantine, your family doctors should be available for advice via telephone if needed.

When it comes to prescription medicines, it may be more difficult to stock up for an emergency. In some cases, insurance restrictions may prevent you from getting any extra medicine. While insurance companies may have valid reasons for limiting how much of certain medications are made available to people, in quarantine situations, some doctors are suggesting having a 30-day supply on hand. It may be that insurance companies will loosen restrictions to allow people to get more medicine, but you should probably ask your doctor about it sooner than later to see what they advise.

Cleaning Supplies

You may have noticed on the back of a can of Lysol, it says that it can kill the human coronavirus among other germs and viruses like the flu. I don't know how conclusive that statement is concerning COVID-19 but the common consensus is that disinfectants can, in fact, kill it where it is living on surfaces. Having plenty of antibiotic soap and other household disinfectants on hand is a must, pandemic or no pandemic. I like to have both Lysol spray and wipes as well as a jug of antibiotic soap to refill dispensers around the house. I'll get more into this later but there are many objects in our houses that are touched multiple times per day by everyone in the household that we simply don't think about throughout a normal day. Having disinfectant spray and wipes to clean those surfaces will help to ensure any virus that may be present there is eliminated.

Don't Forget your Furry Friends!

I probably don't need to remind you if you have pets that they will need extra food, water and medications just like we do; however, in stressful situations, it can be easy sometimes to forget that they will need extra supplies as well. The good news is that most experts have now agreed that our beloved little companions are not likely to catch the virus from humans.

"With so many rich people, only those who don't need money
to be happy are poor."
     (Wesley D'amico)

"Laughter is good for the soul, it is its sunlight, and without
sunlight nothing can live or grow."
     (Wayne Dyer)

Chapter : 17
How Much China Has Lost Due To This Epidemic?

According to a source, it is reported that China has lost around USD60 Billion Dollars during the Wuhan Coronavirus outbreak, and that's a big number. In this moment of economic challenge, China has to act with proper planning to balance out the effect this amount is going to make on its economy.

Even more than the dollars, the loss of people is irreplaceable. The number of deaths from this epidemic have been increasing and is the numbers are increasing at an alarming rate. Some people also think that the numbers are being under-reported, as it is very difficult to differentiate between people who are symptomatic and asymptomatic.

The actual loss from this epidemic is difficult to assess accurately. However, China is trying hard to lower the tensions of a trade war with America by signing trade agreements which will improve its economy. Also, people will be able to get agricultural supplies with both countries lowering tariffs with each other to encourage other countries to continue trade relations with China.

Until a vaccine for the novel coronavirus is found, it is expected that China will face more losses, but still, we have some hope for the vaccine too. As scientists around the world are joining hands to create the first coronavirus vaccine, and it is expected that a vaccine will be available later this year.

Curing the coronavirus

Our only weapon against a virus is our own body. These little soldiers of ours are also referred to as antibodies. These antibodies are formed as an immune response towards hostile bacteria or viruses.

The development of these antibodies keeps taking place in our body whenever we are exposed to a new disease. Most of the time, our body creates antibodies in time and saves us from viruses, but sometimes, the body is unable to form antibodies in time, and forming antibodies becomes more difficult as the patient's condition worsens.

How antibodies save us: The antibodies our bodies create are even smaller than the virus invading our body, and their mode of action is simple. Their duty is to not let them transfer their heredity material to the victim's cells. The cells of the host body when infected, start to reproduce in the millions, resulting in worsening the conditions even more. These antibodies bind to the viruses and destroy their ability to infect the host's cells. In this way, they keep revolving around the body of the victim without affecting him or her.

So, what happens in the case of no formation: In the case of no formation of antibodies, a virus keeps on invading the cells of victims, and eventually, the victim dies because of the problems produced by the constant replication of that virus.

How vaccines are created: The vaccines are nothing more than a virus, but a weakened one. This weak or dead virus is introduced to the body to provoke an immune response against the virus that helps the body in the development of antibodies. The virus is weakened with the help of chemicals or radiation.

These newly produced antibodies are used, when a healthy virus is introduced to the host body, and eventually, the host body shows no sign of illness. Years later, when these antibodies get older, some booster shots are required for more prolonged protection.

Is there is any cure for the Wuhan Coronavirus: Yes, there is a cure, but there is a lot to be done before creating a one-shot solution. Cure for Wuhan Coronavirus is also the same, a weakened virus in the form of a vaccine is needed to save host bodies from becoming infected. Yet still, no vaccine has been created for this type of coronavirus since the virus is relatively new, but some successes are being reported from the researchers in Hong Kong.

Why is difficult to create one vaccine for the whole family: The spikes vary from virus to virus, which allows them to attach with specific host cells. For example, in the case of coronavirus, these host cells are the ones present in the lungs. So, it is virtually impossible to create a single vaccine for all of them, and it is also impossible to create a vaccine without the virus.

Vaccines for the Wuhan Coronavirus: Scientists from Hong Kong reported that they have created a vaccine for the Wuhan Coronavirus, but they are far from using it to treat patients affected with the Wuhan Coronavirus. It is also said that the vaccine is first going to be tested on animals and then on humans, which will take months. So, it is a long way before a good vaccine arrives in the market.

"One day you're gonna wake up and see a beautiful day. It'll be sunny, and everything will be new, changed, clear. What seemed impossible before will become simple, normal. Don't you believe it? I do. And soon. Tomorrow too."

(Fyodor Michajlovič Dostoyevsky)

"Always laugh, laugh, make yourself look crazy, but never sad. Laugh even if the world is falling apart, keep smiling. There are people who live for your smile and others who will gnaw when they realize they couldn't turn it off."

(Roberto Benigni)

Conclusions

Thank you so much for reading "The Pandemics World". It is my hope that you have found the information in this book to be a helpful guide to you in keeping yourself and your family safe from the contagion of a disease that is still being figured out by the medical community at large. Keeping yourself and your family safe and healthy is always the number one priority in life and I commend you for taking steps to be informed and proactive about it.

The information in this book was gathered from valuable resources such as the Red Cross, the Centers for Disease Control and Prevention, the Federal Emergency Management Agency, and the Department of Homeland Security. These reliable sources were used and cited, as their expertise in the control of the spread of disease and the health and wellness of large populations give them great experience to back up those claims.

It is my hope that the information that has been compiled and relayed here for you is helpful to you in keeping yourself and your loved ones safe in the event of a nation or city-wide emergency. It is my hope that the use of this information serves you well and helps you to come through the situation healthier, stronger, and more vital than ever!

No one plans or intends to be the victim of an epidemic disease, but being prepared for any possibility helps to ensure that you're not caught completely unaware, should the unthinkable happen.

Thank you!

...and smile... always smile...